A 30-Day Devotional

Mercy Beyond Measure

Desperate Lives and the Reckless Grace of Jesus

Kurt Salierno & Barry Shafer

Celebrate!

Kurt Salierno

Rom 12:11

InWord *Resources*

Cover Photos: Michael Wilson

Cover Design: Owen Brock, Zender + Associates, Inc.

Published by InWord Resources, Inc.
P.O. Box 531
Middletown, OH 45042
www.inword.org

Printed in the United States of America

ISBN 1-931662-00-2

Library of Congress Control Number 2001090662

09 08 07 06 05 04   9 8 7 6 5 4 3

Contents

Acknowledgements   v
Foreword   vii
How to Use This Book   ix

Introduction   1

Week 1

Day 1   Culture Shock   5
Day 2   Max   15
Day 3   A Bum's Example   23
Day 4   Grandpa   31
Day 5   The Jail   37
Day 6   Do Day   45
Day 7   Worship   47

Week 2

Day 8   The Coat   51
Day 9   Friends   59
Day 10   The Prostitute   63
Day 11   Satan's Pursuit   71
Day 12   Sun Bear   79
Day 13   Do Day   89
Day 14   Worship   91

Week 3

Day 15   The Harmonica   95
Day 16   The Homosexual   109
Day 17   The Dead Man   119
Day 18   Cindy's   125
Day 19   Success   135
Day 20   Do Day   143
Day 21   Worship   145

Week 4

Day 22   Family Pictures   149
Day 23   Everywhere You Look   157
Day 24   Hot Dogs and Beans   163
Day 25   The Night of the Gun   171
Day 26   The College   177
Day 27   Do Day   183
Day 28   Worship   185

Bonus Days

Day 29   Day Away with God   189
Day 30   Say Yes to Mercy   191

Topical Index   193
Scripture Index   194
About the Authors   195

Acknowledgements

From Kurt

A special thank you to Cindy Williams for her dedication to the Lord and willingness to serve Him in any way, which has included helping with this book. The manuscript would not have been finished without the countless hours she spent writing and rewriting each story. Her insight, skill, and devotion to the task were remarkable. Thank you, Cindy. We did it!

Also thank you, Kit Taylor, for the hours spent reading and correcting my grammar and punctuation. Kit's dedication to serving God leaves an eternal stamp on all who are blessed to be touched by her life, and her gift to Jesus was her invaluable help in writing this book.

Cindy and Kit are a great team that made this book possible. If you'd like to use their services for editing or writing, please let me know at www.churchonthestreet.com.

From Barry

Thank you to my wife, Dana, the love and editor of my life, for putting the finishing touches on this project. A big thanks to a special group of teens and young adults who are pursuing with us the measureless mercy and reckless grace of Jesus. They sharpened this book—Andrea Pudel at Hope Community Church in Brampton, Ontario; Cara and Kirby Davis at Christ Presbyterian Church in Nashville, Tennessee; and the youth groups at Breiel Boulevard First Church of God in Middletown, Ohio, and Salem Church of God in Clayton, Ohio.

Foreword

Who wants to marry someone who's been arrested for prostitution? for homosexuality? for public disturbance? And that's just to pick a few! The answer is "me!" But I'd venture to say that the most common answer to that question would be "no one!"

On my first date with a guy named Kurt Salierno, I wasn't quite sure what to think of him. He didn't talk like the other guys. He didn't behave like the other guys either. He didn't even hang around the same places as the other guys I knew. For starters, he stuttered—badly. He also had different ideas about where to take a girl for a date. He didn't even mind hanging around with "bums" on the street.

There was a different story behind this guy, and it intrigued me. So I set out to find the real story and agreed to go on a date with him. We weren't more than a couple of hours into that first date when Kurt asked if I wanted to meet some of his "street friends." I agreed, expecting a movie-like experience, where you watch and learn but don't really come into contact with anything strange.

I was surprised and somewhat scared as Kurt escorted me to places in the city where you don't normally go on a date. But soon I was put at ease. Guys with dirty clothes and breath that reeked of alcohol recognized Kurt right away. They seemed glad to see him on their street. Within a few minutes I realized that Kurt was one of them, while I was an outsider. It wasn't that he was dressed like them or drank what they were drinking; long before that night, Kurt had actually earned the right to talk and share with them. This guy, whom I had only recently met, was a different kind of guy. He loved those smelly and vulgar men. He didn't care that they had problems and had made wrong choices. He knew there was hope for them—and he understood that it was his duty to help them find that hope. After all, wasn't that what our Lord Jesus would want?

Unfortunately, few of us ever understand our obligation to help those who are less fortunate than we are. Few of us want to mix with people different from us. But as believers in Jesus

Christ, God calls us to make a difference in people's lives. He doesn't care whether they smell, dress nicely, or have college degrees. He loves them all just the same. But He **does** care about our hearts and how we respond to His calling.

This book isn't about just learning a new skill or concept. It's about challenging **you** every day. This book is about **real** stories that happen to **real** people. I ask you to read one story and do one Bible study each day, and then stop and listen. What is God telling you? What does He want you to do with that day?

My wish for you may sound a little strange. But what I truly wish is that someday, someone would say about you, "Wow, that guy is weird" or "That girl is strange!" You may not get arrested as Kurt did for helping people in need. But if you do what Jesus wants you to do, people may start saying, "Who would want to marry a guy or a girl like that?" Then, in your quiet times, you can say to yourself, "What a compliment!"

—**Lori Salierno**

How to Use This Book

First off, don't let the calendar format of this book box you in. We chose a four-week cycle to give you a personal study plan that's easy to jump in to. While it's best to move through chronologically—Day 1, Day 2, Day 3, and so on—feel free to do this book at your own pace. You might do a couple of days at a time, or sometimes you may miss a day. The thing is, we know you're up for a challenge—so commit to **owning** this thing for the next 30 days, and see what happens to your life!

Monday through Friday: Personal Reading and Study Time with God
Each day contains a moving story from Kurt and an invigorating search of God's Word from Barry ("Taking It Inward"). You can do the story and the study together in 20–25 minutes.

Saturday: "Do Day"
As you see the power of Jesus' mercy through Kurt's stories and God's Word, it won't take long before you'll want to try it for yourself. Each Saturday is designated as a "Do Day," intended to help you live out the mercy you've read about during the week. We've suggested some ministry activities to get you started, but you'll undoubtedly come up with some great ideas on your own.

Sunday: Worship
Take this book with you to church. The "Worship" page is designed to help you keep listening to God through worship, teaching, and preaching. If you keep your heart soft to God, you'll experience Him weaving your daily study into your worship experience on Sunday.

A Note about "Taking It Inward"

Each Bible study contains a bite-sized chunk of scripture for you to devour. We want you to do more than just read each chunk. In fact, we'll be asking you to look for and mark key details from every passage. (You'll want to round up some colored pencils or a four-color pen before diving in.) God has something specific to say to you in His Word—and the more detail you see, the better your chances of hearing Him clearly. One more thing: We hope these scripture experiences will help you get more out of your Bible than you ever thought possible—and challenge you to have invigorating Bible study for the rest of your life.

Introduction

The stories told here are true accounts of my time spent living with and ministering among those whom society has cast aside—the down and out, the destitute, the homeless. Whether the stories take place on skid row in Portland, the inner city of Atlanta, or on the streets of Phoenix, the need for Jesus is always the same.

This ministry to the homeless started during my freshman year at Warner Pacific College, when I accidentally stumbled onto skid row and led my first "bum" to Christ. Initially I limited my time on the streets to a few hours on Fridays and Saturdays, talking and sharing the love of Jesus with anyone who would listen. Soon, however, as my relationships with these men and women developed, a few hours became two, three, or more nights at a time. Eventually I would spend weeks on the streets, ministering to those who I believe are so precious to God.

There were nights when I slept in garbage bins and warmed my body with rotting garbage. I've slept among "piles" of bodies in order to stay warm enough to survive the Portland ice storms. At times, my life has been in great danger, and I'm certain that it was through God's intervention that I'm alive. I've seen the hopelessness firsthand, but I've also seen the miraculous power of God demonstrated in ways that most Christians today never have the opportunity to experience. For this, I am grateful.

As I travel throughout the country sharing these stories, I'm often asked why I do what I do. To tell you the truth, there have been times when my purpose has become blurred because of the many issues involved with reaching the homeless, along with my own need to secure an income and provide for my family. Yet I continue, certain of my calling to reach out to the unlovely, the drug addicts, the prostitutes, and the drunks. I believe these men and women have as much right to hear about the love of Jesus as you and I. I am convicted and stirred as I read scripture's many accounts of the love and compassion that Jesus, the model for this ministry, showed those whom society had thrown away. I am compelled to do no less.

I realize that not everyone is called to this type of ministry; to many, it may even seem incomprehensible and foolish. So, I bring the streets to you. This book is not about me, but about the persistent love of Jesus and how it can prevail in a world of overwhelming odds. Perhaps as a result of these stories you will be moved to reach beyond what is comfortable and touch someone who might otherwise never have the opportunity to know the love and life-changing power of Jesus Christ. It might be a neighbor or a coworker—or it could be the guy you step over the next time you walk the city streets. This is my prayer.

—KURT SALIERNO

Week 1

Day 1   Culture Shock

Day 2   Max

Day 3   A Bum's Example

Day 4   Grandpa

Day 5   The Jail

Day 6   Do Day

Day 7   Worship

Culture Shock

I stutter. Sometimes just getting my name out is a major ordeal. A simple attempt to introduce myself has caused many to scratch their heads and seriously question my calling into the ministry! Believe me, I understand! I've questioned it a few times myself. Nevertheless, as a young man, I *did* feel the call of God, and I knew the first step I needed to take was to get an education. So, off I went to Warner Pacific College in Portland, Oregon, to answer the call.

Portland was the most incredible city I'd ever seen, and this was the first time in my young life that I had ever been this far from home. Because of my stutter, it was not uncommon for people to think I was mentally handicapped, so this loner from Visalia, California, was overwhelmed at the thought of having to make a whole new group of friends. But I must admit that mixed with my uncertainties was an excited anticipation of this God-appointed adventure.

The fall semester was just ahead, so I got to Portland six weeks early to get settled and find a job. The deserted campus was peaceful, and as I entered the administration building and walked to the admissions office, I could hear my footsteps echo in the empty halls.

"Hi! I'm K-K-K-Kurt S-S-S-Salierno."

The startled admissions clerk had that all too familiar look on her face as I attempted to do what's second nature to practically everyone else—introduce myself. She quickly regained her composure and found my file, which confirmed that I really *was* supposed to be there. Then she smiled, put an "out to lunch" sign on the door, gave me a tour of the campus, and took me to lunch.

MON_{Day} 1

Have I mentioned that I went to Portland without any idea where I would be living or sleeping? My next step, after lunch and a quick look around campus, was to decide where to sleep that night. Standing in the desolate parking lot, surveying all the possibilities, I decided the best one for that night was my car.

About nine o'clock, I noticed some guys across the street sitting on the hoods of their cars. I walked toward them, repeating my name over and over to myself, hoping to make some new friends. So much for first impressions. I watched anxiously as "the look" passed between them while I attempted several times to say "Hi! I'm K-K-K-Kurt." I guess they thought it was easier to ignore me than try to understand me, so they resumed their conversation. The group decided to see a movie downtown, so, acting like one of the guys (and hoping no one would notice I wasn't), I jumped into one of the cars, and off we went. "This is going to be great!" I thought to myself.

I could not believe this city. It was after 9:30 P.M., and people were everywhere—walking, talking, and headed in every direction. My hometown rolled up the sidewalks by this time of night. I must have looked like a kid at his first carnival, trying to take it all in.

We arrived at the theater, and in my eagerness to take in my new surroundings, I never gave a thought to what movie I was paying to see. But as the show started I noticed something unusual about the women on the screen. They were wearing almost nothing.

"Is this a good movie?" I naively whispered to the guy next to me.

"Yeah," he whispered back, "but wait, it gets better!"

Slowly, it hit me. In my zeal to be a part of the group, I'd spent my last few dollars to see an adult movie. My first impulse was to run out of there as fast as my legs would take me. "This isn't a good movie," I said to the guys. "We need to leave!"

The antagonism in my newfound friend's reply was obvious. "Okay, go!" he laughed sarcastically.

Thinking he was surely joking, I tried one more time to make them understand. "I want to leave," I pleaded.

In disbelief, the guys looked at me again and in unison commanded, "Go!"

Trying my best to look pitiable in hopes that someone would feel sorry for me, I walked out. No one followed. As the theater door swung shut behind me, my heart was overwhelmed with loneliness. I felt completely deserted, with nowhere to go and no one to turn to. And I'd foolishly wasted my last few dollars on an adult movie. To make matters worse, even if I had somewhere to go, I didn't have a clue how to get there. Tears stung my eyes as I came to the realization that I was lost in the middle of Portland, with no one to help.

My only recourse was to pray and ask God to guide me. Little did I know, as I cried to Him for help, that He'd already planned to give me heavenly directions back to campus—directions that would change the course of my life forever.

You're probably wondering why I didn't just stop someone for directions, and I did. But I'd barely get the first word out before I'd start to stutter. Then I'd watch in total frustration as any hope of human assistance scurried away, fearing for their lives! Again, I prayed, "Okay, Lord. I'm going to close my eyes and put my arms out in front of me. Stop me when I'm going in the right direction!" I was confident the Lord would direct me. After bumping into a wary couple and scaring them half to death, I stopped, feeling sure of the direction I should go.

I walked what seemed like a mile when I began noticing that the streets had taken on a dreary appearance. A nagging fear began to haunt me. Yet I was sure the Lord had sent me in the right direction, so I kept on. Suddenly a horrible smell stopped me in my tracks. Scanning the streets for the source of the smell, I noticed a man lying in the gutter, and I anxiously crossed over to help him. He was filthy and appeared to have been beaten lifeless. I was certain the stench that permeated him was the smell of death. All my childhood Sunday school lessons about the Good Samaritan flooded back to me, and I knew I had to help him. I began to see firsthand, however, that just like in the Bible story, there were those who simply didn't care.

I looked frantically in every direction for someone to help or to call the police, but I was amazed at the many people who passed by as if nothing unusual had taken place! As my eyes darted around for help, I began to notice another body—and then another. There were fallen bodies everywhere! Perhaps because I was tired or just plain scared, I began to imagine that a cold-blooded killer had shot these helpless people down—and I was the first to stumble onto the grisly scene.

My imagination was working overtime by now, and I was frantic with fear and concern. I ran to find help, praying the police would drive by. Fueled by pure adrenaline, I ran head-on into a man who had just stumbled out of a bar.

"I'm sorry! I didn't mean to run into you." This time the words came *flying* out of my mouth. "Please, Mister, there are a lot of wounded people back there. Can you help me?"

The man stared at me with the same perplexed expression I'd seen earlier in the theater. Sheer panic rose within me, and my thoughts shouted, "Oh, no! He's the one with the gun!" I backed away, apologizing for bothering him and trying nonchalantly to walk away.

My wild imagination waited for the man to pull his gun and shoot me in the back. My entire body tensed, anticipating the fatal shot that would end my life. I wanted to run, but fearing that my sudden movement might alarm the shooter even more, I forced my feet to walk.

Suddenly, I heard the man yell, "Hey, boy, come here!"

My heart was in my throat, but I knew if I ran I was a dead man. My shoes felt like concrete blocks as I turned to face my executioner. For the second time that night, tears welled up in my eyes as I prepared to meet Jesus face to face. The man walked slowly to me, cocked his head to one side, and looked at me as if I had three heads. "What you need is a drink!" he said. "Come on with me."

Sure he would shoot me if I refused—and hoping to add a few more minutes to my fleeting existence—I swallowed the lump in my throat, uttered a barely discernable "okay," and followed him into the bar.

Until that moment, my experience with the inside of a bar was limited to what I had seen on television. But nothing I'd ever seen on TV had prepared me for the reality of the dirt and filth in this place. It was a dungeon of darkness and despair. To my dismay, I found more men inside the bar who appeared to be dead! They were lying on the floor or slumped in chairs, and each one possessed the now familiar death-stench. "This man is a maniac," I thought.

My escort led me to a table and asked what I wanted to drink. "I'll have a water," I replied. He found this curiously amusing.

"Come on, kid, get something stronger," he ordered.

"Okay, I'll take a Coke."

Shaking his head, he ordered his drink. Then he leaned back in his chair and asked in bewilderment, "What's a kid like you doing in a place like this?"

By now I was stuttering so badly that with every attempt to speak, I resembled a yard sprinkler that sprays everything in its path! Taking a deep breath, I attempted to answer the man's question while he held a napkin over his face for protection. I told him that I came to Portland from a small town in California. I began to explain my calling into the ministry and my decision to attend Warner Pacific College in preparation. As we talked, it became clear to me that this man was not responsible for the mayhem I'd discovered outside. So I told him about the condition of the men I'd seen lying on the streets and related the details of the heinous crime I had envisioned taking place.

"Those men weren't shot," he laughed. "They were drunk and passed out! This is skid row." The relief I felt was short-lived as I fully realized the sad truth of what he'd just said.

We talked for more than two hours that night, and the man seemed as intrigued with me as I was with him. How ironic that my first friend in this strange new place would be a skid row bum! He seemed to get such a kick out of my stuttering and asked me how in the world I was going to be able to preach when I could hardly talk. "Good question," I thought to myself. I explained to my friend that if God called me to do it, I would trust Him to work out the details.

"But how can you trust someone you can't even see?" he asked.

In our short time together, I was able to explain the love of God to this man and share my testimony with him. "I'm proof," I said, "that God will not let us down when we align the direction of our lives with His." It was quite obvious that our time together was God-appointed, and I found myself asking if he'd like to invite Christ into his life. To my complete amazement, he reached across the table, grabbed my hands, and asked, "Do you think God would direct my life like He has yours?" I assured him that He would. After more conversation, in a dark, dismal den of the Enemy himself, that skid row bum asked Jesus Christ to be his Lord and Savior.

As we said our good-byes, my new brother in Christ pointed me in the direction of campus. I prayed for him as I walked, thanking God for the detour and for allowing me to participate in the miracle that had just taken place. The sun was rising as I arrived back at school, but instead of fatigue, I felt such incredible joy. That's when I realized that if one man on skid row desired to know Jesus, there had to be more—and I needed to find them.

Taking It Inward

Have you ever had a moment like Kurt's—when the theater door slammed shut behind him and none of his friends followed him out? Theater exit doors usually don't have handles on the outside, so at that moment all of Kurt's options seemed closed.

For you, it may have been bad news from a doctor, a divorce in your family, or the loss of a close friend. You probably felt confusion, loneliness, even despair—emotions you thought couldn't possibly lead to anything good.

Hagar was a woman in the Bible who felt a door slam behind her, too. One of the world's first single moms, Hagar was a victim of circumstances beyond her control. Her story is an awesome example of how God intervenes and directs in moments when we have no answers.

In Genesis 12, God promised Abram (later called Abraham) that he would be the father of a great nation. Knowing that he and his wife, Sarai, were way past their child-bearing years, Abram couldn't trust God's plan. So he and Sarai took things into their own hands—and made a total mess. That's where we pick up the action.

Read about Hagar in the Bible passage below. God doesn't want you to miss the detail, so try this: As you read, circle every mention of Hagar with a colored pen or pencil. Draw a cloud [☁] around every mention of the Lord or His angel.

Genesis 16:1–14

[1] Now Sarai, Abram's wife, had borne him no children. But she had an Egyptian maidservant named Hagar; [2] so she said to Abram, "The LORD has kept me from having children. Go, sleep with my maidservant; perhaps I can build a family through her." Abram agreed to what Sarai said. [3] So after Abram had been living in Canaan ten years, Sarai his wife took her Egyptian maidservant Hagar and gave her to her husband to be his wife. [4] He slept with Hagar, and she conceived. When she knew she was pregnant, she began to despise her mistress.

MON_{Day} 1

⁵ Then Sarai said to Abram, "You are responsible for the wrong I am suffering. I put my servant in your arms, and now that she knows she is pregnant, she despises me. May the LORD judge between you and me." ⁶ "Your servant is in your hands," Abram said. "Do with her whatever you think best." Then Sarai mistreated Hagar; so she fled from her.

⁷ The angel of the LORD found Hagar near a spring in the desert; it was the spring that is beside the road to Shur. ⁸ And he said, "Hagar, servant of Sarai, where have you come from, and where are you going?" "I'm running away from my mistress Sarai," she answered. ⁹ Then the angel of the LORD told her, "Go back to your mistress and submit to her." ¹⁰ The angel added, "I will so increase your descendants that they will be too numerous to count." ¹¹ The angel of the LORD also said to her: "You are now with child and you will have a son. You shall name him Ishmael, for the LORD has heard of your misery. ¹² He will be a wild donkey of a man; his hand will be against everyone and everyone's hand against him, and he will live in hostility toward all his brothers." ¹³ She gave this name to the LORD who spoke to her: "You are the God who sees me," for she said, "I have now seen the One who sees me." ¹⁴ That is why the well was called Beer Lahai Roi; it is still there, between Kadesh and Bered.

The similarities between Hagar's situation and Kurt's are striking. Both were cast out, lonely, and confused. And in the most unlikely moment, God intervened. Take a moment to look at the clouds you marked, and list below everything you learn about the Lord and His angel. Make your list as detailed as possible.

The Lord

Did you notice the two instructions God gave to help Hagar deal with the situation? (Hint: See verse 9.) Write these instructions here.

1.

2.

How did Hagar describe God after encountering Him? Find this (it's near the end of the passage). Then write out word-for-word Hagar's description of God.

Kurt and Hagar are separated in time by thousands of years, but God's intervention is the same! Not only did God **not** whisk them out of their dilemmas, He asked that they walk with Him into the fire. Hagar heard the words, "Return and submit." Kurt heard, "Hey, boy, come here!" And God used their responsiveness to do something big in their lives—bigger than either could imagine.

Seal the Deal

What's going on in your life right now? Is there anything to which God is calling you to "return and submit"? What pain or struggles are you experiencing? Remember, these could be God's way of preparing you for something. Write your thoughts in the space below.

My Pain/Struggles   **What God Might Be Prepping Me For**

Spend a moment in worship, declaring to God that He is "the God who sees." Read the verses below from your Bible. Then, according to these verses, write down anything good that results from trouble.

2 Corinthians 1:3–5

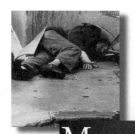

Max

They told me on the streets to stay away from the man they called Max. They said he was dangerous and that he'd even killed people. So I tried to avoid him and was successful—until late one night.

I was looking for a garbage bin to sleep in, and I found one; the heavy lid propped open with a rock created an opening just large enough to allow air to circulate. I opened the top and began to climb in. As I did, I stepped on a person's head. It was Max's.

"I'm sorry," I quickly apologized.

"Who are you!" he demanded.

"My name is "K-K-K—"

I didn't have time to get my name out before he hollered, "You're the preacher boy, aren't you? Get out of here, preacher boy!"

I tried to climb out of the garbage bin and had one foot inside and one foot out, when Max said, "No, wait! Get back in here." With much trepidation, I climbed back in and sat down among the rotting garbage, less than twelve inches from the notorious Max.

"So, you're the one who keeps talking about this Jesus. You don't really believe that crazy stuff, do you?" He used some expletives I can't repeat.

"Yes," I replied, "I really do believe in Him, and He's given His life for me because He loves me. And you know what? He loves you."

Bam! Max slammed my head against the side of the garbage bin. "Don't tell me about His love. Nobody loves me. Now get out of this garbage can!" And I did...quickly.

A few nights later, I was walking down the street and heard a man behind me yell, "Hey, preacher!" Recognizing the voice as Max's, I turned and immediately apologized for being on his side of the street. "No, wait!" he yelled. "Tell me about this *God*. Who is He?"

I told Max that God loved him so much that He sent His Son Jesus to this earth. While He was here, Jesus gave His life to pay the price for all of the bad things Max had ever done. Suddenly Max grabbed the neck of my shirt, and slamming me against the building where we stood, he demanded, "How do you know what I've done?"

"Well, I've heard about you on the streets, but no matter what you've done, God can forgive you. He loves you."

The next thing I knew, the back of Max's hand struck my face. He glared at me a moment in silence, then turned to walk away. I stood looking after him, rubbing my sore jaw and thinking, "Okay, God, this is a tough one, but I'm willing to do whatever it takes to lead this man to You."

The next day I heard Max hollering, "Preacher, come over here!" Touching my jaw, which still ached from our previous encounter, I crossed the street. Max looked to his left and right to make sure no one was nearby, which I'll admit made me very uneasy. I had no idea what to expect from this man. Then, quietly, as if on some covert mission, he indicated for me to sit down with him on the sidewalk. He was ready to talk about Jesus.

Max had so many questions, and I explained in great detail how Jesus Christ came to earth to die for his sins. I told him that even if he were the only man on earth, Jesus would have died just for him.

Max's response was a mix of anger and hopelessness. He exploded, "I'm just a bum! I'm no good, and I've hurt and killed people. Jesus wouldn't do that for me." I assured him that He already had. "That was a long time ago," Max said. "Jesus didn't even know about me then."

Shaking my head I replied, "Max, He had you on His mind when He died."

Suddenly Max's resolve crumbled and his countenance changed. Tears began to stream down his tired, battered face. He grabbed my shirt with both hands and pulled me so close that I could feel his hot alcohol breath on my face. Through clenched teeth he said, "Are you certain there is a God?"

Looking him in the eyes, I replied, "Max, He's here. Can't you feel Him?"

"Are you *certain* there's a God?" His words were fueled by pure desperation, and he searched my face for any indication that what I said was really possible. By now, his tears were a steady flow.

"Max." I spoke softly now, my voice heavy with compassion for this broken man. "You can feel Him, can't you? You've been fighting Him all your life, but you know He's here. He loves you, Max, and I love you. That's why I'm here."

Slowly he loosened his grip on my shirt and asked, "How much does He want? How much does He want to get this love?"

I answered, "It's free, Max. It's free. He's already paid the price."

He asked, "Well, what do I do?" I explained to Max how to receive the free gift of God's grace, and as we held hands, Max invited Jesus Christ into his life.

When we finished praying and opened our eyes, I saw a new man where the old Max used to be. His face looked different. The hard lines etched by hatred and anger had already been softened by the tender touch of God. He was a new man inside and out. The roughest guy on the street was now a believer.

Taking It Inward

The message of the gospel—in its purest form—can be irresistible. This explains why hardened, unlikely candidates like Max often have a natural curiosity about the things Jesus said and did.

When Jesus ministered on earth, there was a man named Nicodemus who was a lot like Max—hardened toward the message of Jesus and an unlikely candidate to follow Him. Nicodemus was a member of the Pharisees, a Jewish sect that, in short, hated Jesus. Nicodemus made three appearances in the gospel of John, the only gospel to mention him.

All three passages that mention Nicodemus are printed below. As you read these verses, make notes in the right-hand margin of everything that gives you a clue about Nicodemus's attitude toward Jesus.

Early in Jesus' Ministry—John 3:1–16

Notes

1 Now there was a man of the Pharisees named Nicodemus, a member of the Jewish ruling council. 2 He came to Jesus at night and said, "Rabbi, we know you are a teacher who has come from God. For no one could perform the miraculous signs you are doing if God were not with him." 3 In reply Jesus declared, "I tell you the truth, no one can see the kingdom of God unless he is born again." 4 "How can a man be born when he is old?" Nicodemus asked. "Surely he cannot enter a second time into his mother's womb to be born!"

5 Jesus answered, "I tell you the truth, no one can enter the kingdom of God unless he is born of water and the Spirit. 6 Flesh gives birth to flesh, but the Spirit gives birth to spirit. 7 You should not be surprised at my saying, 'You must be born again.' 8 The wind blows wherever it pleases. You hear its sound, but you cannot tell where it comes from or where it is going. So it is with everyone born of the Spirit." 9 "How can this be?" Nicodemus asked.

¹⁰ "You are Israel's teacher," said Jesus, "and do you not understand these things? ¹¹ I tell you the truth, we speak of what we know, and we testify to what we have seen, but still you people do not accept our testimony. ¹² I have spoken to you of earthly things and you do not believe; how then will you believe if I speak of heavenly things? ¹³ No one has ever gone into heaven except the one who came from heaven—the Son of Man. ¹⁴ Just as Moses lifted up the snake in the desert, so the Son of Man must be lifted up, ¹⁵ that everyone who believes in him may have eternal life. ¹⁶ "For God so loved the world that he gave his one and only Son, that whoever believes in him shall not perish but have eternal life.

Notes

Later in Jesus' Ministry—John 7:43–53

⁴³ Thus the people were divided because of Jesus. ⁴⁴ Some wanted to seize him, but no one laid a hand on him. ⁴⁵ Finally the temple guards went back to the chief priests and Pharisees, who asked them, "Why didn't you bring him in?" ⁴⁶ "No one ever spoke the way this man does," the guards declared.

⁴⁷ "You mean he has deceived you also?" the Pharisees retorted. ⁴⁸ "Has any of the rulers or of the Pharisees believed in him? ⁴⁹ No! But this mob that knows nothing of the law—there is a curse on them." ⁵⁰ Nicodemus, who had gone to Jesus earlier and who was one of their own number, asked, ⁵¹ "Does our law condemn anyone without first hearing him to find out what he is doing?" ⁵² They replied, "Are you from Galilee, too? Look into it, and you will find that a prophet does not come out of Galilee." ⁵³ Then each went to his own home.

Just Moments after Jesus' Death—John 19:38–42

³⁸ Later, Joseph of Arimathea asked Pilate for the body of Jesus. Now Joseph was a disciple of Jesus, but secretly because he feared the Jews. With Pilate's permission, he came and took the body away. ³⁹ He was accompanied by Nicodemus, the man who earlier had visited Jesus at night. Nicodemus

TUE_{Day} 2

> brought a mixture of myrrh and aloes, about seventy-five pounds. [40] Taking Jesus' body, the two of them wrapped it, with the spices, in strips of linen. This was in accordance with Jewish burial customs. [41] At the place where Jesus was crucified, there was a garden, and in the garden a new tomb, in which no one had ever been laid. [42] Because it was the Jewish day of Preparation and since the tomb was nearby, they laid Jesus there.

Notes

What do you think? Did Jesus' first meeting with Nicodemus have an effect? Go back to their first meeting in John 3, and reread what Jesus said to Nicodemus, especially verses 5–8. Then check the words below that describe Jesus' approach in sharing the gospel with Nicodemus.

☐ direct
☐ sugar-coated
☐ vague

☐ timid
☐ bold

How would you describe Nicodemus's spiritual condition when he first met up with Jesus?

☐ curious
☐ confrontational

☐ seeking
☐ apathetic

Is there anyone in your life who might be a Nicodemus—cautiously curious about the gospel? Remember, the first criterion is that he or she may be someone you'd never expect to be interested in God (like Max). Take a minute to list these people below.

Now spend some time praying for them, using the prayers in the verses on the next page as your guide. Pray these prayers word-for-word and substitute the names on your list for words like "you." See what happens when you pray for these people **every day** for the next seven days!

Ephesians 1:17–21   **Colossians 1:9–14**

After you've prayed, expect curiosity from these people! You've just read about two people who seemed very hardened to the gospel—yet they broke the ice themselves with their probing, curious comments. Nicodemus said, "Rabbi, we know you are a teacher who has come from God." Max said, "Tell me about this **God**." So expect curiosity and be ready to respond.

Seal the Deal

Want to see something cool? Compare Jesus' and Kurt's responses to their skeptical friends. For Jesus' response, see John 3:10–16; for Kurt's, find Max's cynical command, "Tell me about this **God**. Who is He?"—then read the next line.

A Bum's Example

What priceless lessons I've learned from the bums and prostitutes living on the streets. What a blessing it's been to witness broken lives being transformed by the power of God. The examples of servanthood and sacrifice set by some of these folks have set me back on my heels. I'm certain they would cause even the most pious servant of God to stand amazed.

One unforgettable example of Christ's love was set for me through Max. You'll remember that after months of witnessing, sometimes under very harrowing circumstances, I had the privilege of seeing Max come to know Jesus Christ as his Lord and Savior. Along with the miracle of salvation, God seemed to have placed in Max a deep understanding of what it meant to share in Christ's suffering. I soon discovered that I had much to learn from this skid row bum.

It was January in downtown Portland, and the weather conditions were ripe for one of Portland's infamous ice storms. These storms create extreme danger for those living on the streets; unless one is lucky enough to find shelter, there is no place to hide from the devastation. When an ice storm is approaching, the smartest thing to do is to find a shelter before all available space is taken, leaving others, quite literally, out in the cold.

As the temperature began to drop on that dreary, rain-soaked January day, Max and I searched out and located a shelter that still had some availability. I was grateful as we took our place in line and began to anticipate the reprieve from the rain and ice that was sure to follow. Slowly, with Max right behind me, I worked my way to the front of the line. But as I eagerly stepped inside the shelter, Max grabbed my arm.

"Max, come on," I said impatiently. "Let's get in before there's no more space. It's freezing out here, and it's only going to get worse."

Max just stood there holding my arm and asked, "But if Jesus were here, wouldn't He let those other guys go first?"

I didn't know how to respond. I was so cold, and I knew that surviving this storm without shelter would be nearly impossible. I looked at Max, then at the long line of guys behind us in the freezing rain, then back at Max again.

"Well," I stammered, "umm, maybe. Yeah, that's what He'd do."

So Max and I stood back and let the other men go in before us. Helplessly I watched as the shelter filled to capacity and the doors closed in our faces.

With no time to lose, we began our frantic search for another shelter, then another. Each time, Max did the same thing. He'd step back and wait for the other men to go in first. To be completely honest, I wasn't as anxious as he to set Christ's example. Gripped by the realization that I might die in this storm, my mind was less on the other men than on my own survival. I knew, however, that Max was right, so I stayed with him.

Finally, we stood on the threshold of the only shelter left open that night. Max grabbed me as I started to walk in. "Look at the line," he said. "Shouldn't we let the other guys go first? Isn't that what Jesus would do?" I looked with longing inside the warm building at the multitude of men already snuggling into their blanket-cocoons for the night.

With a half grin, I sheepishly answered, "Well, Max, I think He would have seen this as a great opportunity to go in and witness to all those guys. What do you think?"

Chuckling and shaking his head, he answered, "No, He wouldn't. He'd let these guys go in first, too."

I looked at Max's worn face, his eyes sparkling with the love of Jesus, and stepped aside. Within a few minutes the doors closed for the night, shutting out our last hope for safety and shelter from the storm.

The rain gradually changed to ice and painfully stung our skin as we searched the deserted streets for some type of covering from the elements. Eventually, we stumbled onto a cubbyhole and began to adorn ourselves with the winter wardrobe of the homeless. First we scavenged for old newspapers and rotting food to stuff inside our shirts and pants for insulation. Then, along with the few others who couldn't get into a shelter, we formed a human "pile" by layering ourselves on top of one another. Squeezing together like that allowed us to use our combined body heat to stay warm—although the top man had to absorb the brunt of the pelting ice and cold. Every hour or so, we'd rotate our positions in the pile so that the same man wasn't always on top.

That night we squirmed and pushed against each other until we each became comfortable enough to catch a few hours of sleep. The smell of stale alcohol and rotting garbage was hard to stomach, but it was better than the alternative. Somehow I managed to fall asleep.

"Hey, get off me!"

I awoke the next morning to the voices of grumpy, cold men as the pile of bodies came to life. The layer of ice began to crack as we freed ourselves from the tangle of humanity. The morning sun felt gloriously warm on my face, and I looked around to survey the destruction created by the terrible storm. Unable to remember ever having moved, I wondered who the unlucky men were who got stuck on the top of the pile throughout the night.

I stood to stretch my stiff body and overheard someone mention a bar down the street that was serving coffee. "Let's go," I said, reaching for Max's hand to help him up off the cold sidewalk. I pulled him up, but as I let go, he fell right back down.

"Come on, Max, quit playing around. My back hurts, I'm cold, and I want to go somewhere and warm up."

Max just looked at me, smiled, and said, "Hey, we made it, didn't we?"

My impatience was obvious in my reply. "Yeah, Max, we sure did. Now, come on!" I grabbed his hand and pulled him up again, only to watch him fall as soon as I let go. I knelt to look at him and realized he wasn't wearing any shoes.

"Max, where are your shoes? What'd you do with your shoes?" My voice was a mixture of grave concern and annoyance.

"Well, there was a man walking down the street late last night," he explained, "and he had holes in his shoes. I knew he'd never make it like that, so I gave him mine. That's what Jesus would have done, wouldn't He?"

I looked at him in complete disbelief. "Max, you crazy bum!" I reached down and touched his feet and toes, causing him to shudder with pain. That's when I asked him where he had slept all night. He told me he'd stayed on top of the pile because he didn't want any of the other guys to be exposed. He was sure that was what Jesus would have done.

"I didn't want the ice to settle on you guys," he said. The sincerity and love in his voice broke my heart. I left Max on the sidewalk while I ran to call the police. Several agonizing hours later they arrived and took him to the hospital.

I looked for Max's return each day. Finally, one sunny afternoon, I spotted him on a street corner. Running to where he was, I asked, "Max, how are you doing? Are you all right? Where have you—?"

The words stuck in my throat as I got close enough to see bandages where his feet used to be. Severe frostbite and gangrene had set in, necessitating the amputation of both of Max's feet.

I stuttered and stammered as I searched for words to convey my grief over his terrible condition. Smiling from ear to ear, Max looked at me and said, "Yeah, but we made it, didn't we? We made it."

Max seemed to be in constant pain, but instead of complaining, he asked me to read to him from the Bible about Jesus and what He had done for him. He loved the story of the cross. He loved the fact that at any moment, Jesus could have commanded the angels to slaughter His accusers. He could have cried out, "Enough! I'm done loving. It's too hard!" Max was amazed that Christ loved us so much that He endured all that suffering. He touched my arm and said, "Read that part to me again from John, where it says in the same way Christ loved us, we are to love each other." With tears threatening to spill down my cheeks, I read the verses, awed by the depth of this man's love for those around him.

Max made several more trips to the hospital as the pain and gangrene continued to ravage his body. Each time, the doctors would amputate more, then send him out on the streets to heal. I couldn't imagine the pain this man endured, but his face shone with the serenity of one who knew there were better things waiting for him in heaven. He'd ask me over and over to read to him about Jesus, and he'd smile as the words reminded him of the price Jesus had paid for him on the cross.

One afternoon, an officer pulled up by the curb and rolled down his window. This usually wasn't a good sign, so I turned to walk away. The officer yelled after me, "Hey, you! Come back here!"

Turning around, I pointed to myself as if to say, "You mean me?"

He nodded his head. "Yeah, you. Aren't you the one who hung around with the guy with no legs?"

I told him I was and asked if everything was okay.

"Well, he's dead," the officer replied.

My heart sank and tears filled my eyes. "Max," I thought. "Oh, Max."

The officer continued, "But wait. That's not what I wanted to tell you. There was something different about that guy." He proceeded to tell me of a night when the hospital was full from top to bottom with people who'd been injured in the ice storm and were suffering from various injuries. People were lying everywhere, miserable, except for Max.

"The guy with no legs was wheeling himself around in his wheelchair, making people laugh and trying to encourage them." The officer continued, shaking his head in amazement, "There was something different about that guy." Rolling up his window, he drove off.

As I walked away slowly, I envisioned Max in heaven, running around on two strong legs. I saw him jumping and shouting praise to his Savior. I couldn't help but look back at the man he once was, so full of hatred and bitterness. The officer's words echoed in my mind: "There was something different about that guy."

I smiled and shook my head. "Yes," I thought. "It was Jesus."

Taking It Inward

Have you ever thought that Jesus' radical commands were too far-fetched to take seriously? Go two miles with someone when you're asked to go one…give away the coat off your back, as well as your shirt…turn one cheek when the other's been slapped. **Yeah, right.** You may even have thought, "Does anybody really do stuff like that?" As you saw in the story of Max—**yes!**

With Jesus, a lifestyle of sacrifice should be the norm—not the exception. And amazing things happen when we live this way. Just before Jesus' crucifixion, He had an intimate talk with His disciples about how to live sacrificially with each other and the world around them. Here are two excerpts from that conversation between Jesus and His disciples. Incidentally, they're the very words that motivated Max to love as Jesus loved! As you read these verses, draw a heart [♡] over every mention of the word "love." Remember that it's Jesus who's speaking in each passage.

John 13:34–35

34 "A new command I give you: Love one another. As I have loved you, so you must love one another. 35 By this all men will know that you are my disciples, if you love one another."

John 15:10–14

10 "If you obey my commands, you will remain in my love, just as I have obeyed my Father's commands and remain in his love. 11 I have told you this so that my joy may be in you and that your joy may be complete. 12 My command is this: Love each other as I have loved you. 13 Greater love has no one than this, that he lay down his life for his friends. 14 You are my friends if you do what I command."

Now look back at the hearts you've drawn. Find out everything you can about love by looking for the answers to these questions. Be sure to write what you find in the space provided.

1. Who is to do the loving?

2. Whom are we to love?

3. To what degree are we to love? (Hint: Look for the word "as"!)

Mercy Beyond Measure – **A Bum's Example**

4. What will result from this type of love? (This is big!)

5. What is God stressing to you through these two passages?

Killer question: Can people look at your love for others and declare, "You **must** be a disciple of Jesus!" This is what Jesus said would happen if we loved the way He did. What needs to change in your life in order for this to happen?

Seal the Deal

Max taught us a lot about sacrificial love. But what about you? Are you loving people "to the Max" (pun intended)? Think of one act of sacrificial love you can do by tomorrow, and write it here: _____. **Then do it!** If you need any more motivation on the subject, check out 1 John 4:7–15.

Grandpa

treet people are a paradox. At times they're loners, struggling to protect themselves and to simply survive. Other times they show great concern and care for one another. I've had the opportunity to experience their benevolence firsthand on several occasions.

One wintry night, I began shivering uncontrollably, and no matter what I did, I could not get warm. The cold air had reached its icy fingers inside my inadequate jacket and chilled me to the bone. Sitting among us was an old man I'd seen around a few times and had heard referred to as "Grandpa." He noticed how badly I was shivering and invited me to take a walk with him to get warm.

As the old man led me down the streets, I began to imagine where we might end up. It could be just about anywhere. Finally, we walked behind a factory and came upon a garbage bin, apparently our predetermined destination. The old man quickly went about his work of making me warm for the night. I watched as he retrieved newspaper from the garbage bin and expertly rolled each piece. Like a man on a mission, he ordered me to unbutton my jacket. Noting the puzzled look on my face, he added, "It's okay. Trust me."

Grandpa stuffed my jacket full of the rolled newspaper until I looked like a human scarecrow. The sleeves of my jacket were so stiff with the paper that spilled out over my hands that I could barely bend my arms. But I was warm that night for the first time.

Next the old man invited me to share his garbage bin for the night. What an honor! Now, you might scratch your head and wonder why in the world I'd consider being invited into a garbage bin full of rotting garbage so special. But on the streets, this gesture is the equivalent of being invited into someone's home. I felt honored and accepted.

THU_{Day} 4

We climbed into the garbage bin, pushing and maneuvering the garbage until we had snuggled in comfortably. Then we piled the garbage around us for added insulation from the cold. Just as we settled in for the night, the debris at the other end of the garbage bin began to move. Before I had a chance to discover what caused the movement, up popped a man's head!

"That's Charlie," the old man said. "He's a good guy. He's family." Nodding in my direction, he told Charlie, "This here's 'The Kid.' He's a good boy." This simple expression of acceptance warmed my heart as the garbage warmed my body. The old man had welcomed me into his world.

The following morning became a training session in street survival. The old man decided to teach me the ropes. That day I learned where to hide if the police were in pursuit, what alleys blocked the cold wind, and where the closest Salvation Army mission was located. He showed me what garbage cans provided the best breakfast, lunch, and supper to be had on the streets. Grandpa had a plan of survival for every conceivable situation!

I didn't see much of the old man again until several nights later, when the unusually quiet night was shattered by the sound of screeching tires and a blaring car horn. I turned just in time to see the car barely miss the body of a man lying in the middle of the street. It was Grandpa. The car swerved and stopped. Once the driver realized the body was that of a street bum, he drove on, his irritation obvious. I rushed to the old man and noticed the shattered bottle next to his hand. It had apparently broken when he fell. I quickly scooped him up in my arms and returned to the sidewalk. His clothes were soaking wet, and his body felt like ice. I knew if I didn't get him into dry clothes and a shelter, he would die.

I remembered a place that Grandpa and I had passed once and that he'd referred to it as home. So I quickly headed that direction, having no idea who would answer when I pounded on the heavy wooden door so late at night. Minutes later, the door cracked open enough to reveal a suspicious eye. A voice shouted, "Go away!" and the door slammed in my face. I knocked again. This time an angry man opened the door wide and explained to me, using some creative language, that I was not welcome there. But he suddenly fell silent when he recognized the lifeless form in my arms.

"Where did you find Grandpa?" he asked as he beckoned me in. "We've been worried about him."

As he ushered me inside, I saw that "home" to Grandpa was a vast, warehouse-like room with men lying on the floor, some in sleeping bags and others wrapped in blankets. The floor was filled to capacity on this blustery night.

"We usually don't let anyone in this late," my host told me as we began to peel off Grandpa's wet clothing. "When the floor fills up, I lock the door."

Pointing in the direction of the wall, he told me, "Get the sleeping bag out of the cubbyhole marked 'Grandpa.'" The wall was covered from top to bottom with one-foot-square cubicles, each identified by someone's name. Sure enough, there was Grandpa's cubby. I unfolded the old man's sleeping bag and smiled to myself at its childish design of pink happy faces.

We tucked the old man in, and I felt relieved to know he had this place to come to. It was "home" to him—a place where someone obviously cared about him. I wondered who provided this simple, necessary place of security and warmth for the hundred or so men huddled on the floor. It could have been a businessman, the government, or a church.

To whomever it was, I felt grateful for the shelter and safety they'd provided to the "insignificant ones" living in the streets. This time it was neither garbage nor newspaper that warmed me. The warmth I felt came straight from my heart.

Taking It Inward

To be honest, Grandpa's first inclination may not have been to invite the shivering Kurt along for a walk. When you're scraping for your own safety and resources, you don't want the added pressure of looking out for someone else's welfare. But that didn't stop him—and it shouldn't stop us either.

God created us to enjoy relationships with other people. We're wired to respond to encouragement, gratitude, and a helping hand. Use your imagination to picture Grandpa leading Kurt through the streets, stuffing newspapers inside his jacket, inviting him into a garbage bin, and looking out for his welfare. With these images in your mind, read the passages below. To help you read God's Word carefully, underline anything that reminds you of the friendship Kurt and Grandpa shared. Then, in the margin, write out any phrases that:

- explain why it's good to look out for each other;
- instruct or command us to look out for each other.

Ecclesiastes 4:9–10

9 Two are better than one, because they have a good return for their work: 10 If one falls down, his friend can help him up. But pity the man who falls and has no one to help him up!

Romans 12:10–13

10 Be devoted to one another in brotherly love. Honor one another above yourselves. 11 Never be lacking in zeal, but keep your spiritual fervor, serving the Lord. 12 Be joyful in hope, patient in affliction, faithful in prayer. 13 Share with God's people who are in need. Practice hospitality.

Hebrews 13:1–3

1 Keep on loving each other as brothers. 2 Do not forget to entertain strangers, for by so doing some people have entertained angels without knowing it. 3 Remember those in prison as if you were their fellow prisoners, and those who are mistreated as if you yourselves were suffering.

Take a minute to write down some names of people you know—people who you suspect may be alone. Maybe it's someone new in town—or who just lost a loved one or has no family close by. If no names come to mind right away, ask the Lord to place someone on your heart.

With these names in mind, meditate on the verses you just read. Give God a chance to prompt your heart about helping the people around you who are in need. As you meditate on these verses, circle any specific instructions that stand out to you. If the Lord places something on your mind, write it here.

Seal the Deal

Don't go on to the next chapter before showing hospitality to someone in need! The instructions you've seen in scripture are things you can do anytime, anywhere!

You may have noticed that Grandpa was rewarded for extending hospitality to Kurt. When the tables were turned and he was the one in need, Kurt was there to "help him up" (to borrow a phrase from Ecclesiastes). The promises of God are true; we can trust His Word. Let that motivate you to obey what He says!

The Jail

I've had a few run-ins with the police, usually because I was in the wrong place at the wrong time. At first the officers assumed I was just another derelict, probably because I looked like one—and after having slept a few nights in heaps of garbage, I smelled like one, too! They soon learned, however, that I didn't have to be there, but rather chose to be in order to minister to the men and women living on the streets. This made them no more sympathetic toward me when trouble broke out. I was just one more street person to contend with, regardless of my noble reasons for being there.

One evening an angry drunk man came by the place where I stood talking with some of the bums. For no apparent reason, he swung a bottle, hitting one of the men, slicing his head open, and causing a minor riot to ensue. I stayed around to help the injured man and ended up in the police paddy wagon with everyone else.

One of the officers on the scene had tried many times to discourage me from hanging around the bums. He felt it was just too dangerous. As we arrived at the police station, I could see him talking to the other officers; though I couldn't hear their conversation, I knew it was about me and that it probably wasn't good.

This wasn't my first arrest. Several times before I'd been mistaken as having been part of some disturbance. But this was the first time they decided to lock me up to teach me a lesson. Though I was only trying to help the injured, I found myself in the "drunk tank." In the darkness, I felt my way down the wall and sat on the floor, which was cold and wet with urine and vomit from the drunks sharing my cell.

"How disgusting!" I thought. "What in the world am I doing here?" Overcome with self-pity, I complained silently, "Lord, there are other people who could do this kind of ministry. Why me?"

Nothing happens by accident with God in control, and that night was no exception. As I sat against the wall arguing with God, explaining all the reasons I shouldn't be there, some of the men began to talk. "Oh, great," I thought. "The last thing I want right now is to get into a discussion with a bunch of drunks!" So I sat there listening, trying not to be involved.

As I listened, I learned that two of the men had homes and families. They'd been out buying cheap booze when the fight broke out, and now they were in jail, worrying about how upset their wives were going to be. These men were middle aged and well dressed. All kinds of people end up on the streets.

"Why are *you* here?" one of the men asked, pointing in my direction. "You're not drunk!"

"Like you, I was in the wrong place at the wrong time. I was standing on the street corner with a bunch of the guys when the fight broke out." The self-pity in my voice must have been obvious. I decided to get up and join the two men.

Trying hard to see me in the dark cell, the man asked, "Are you the preacher boy?" Perplexed by the question, I shook my head, no. I told them my name and explained that I was on the streets to show the men and women living there an alternative way to live through the power and love of Jesus Christ.

"Well, then you *are* the preacher boy!" the man said. Chuckling, I asked him to explain. "There's talk on the streets about a kid who lives here and likes to talk about Jesus. The word is that if you want to get your ear talked off, find him."

"Well, I do tend to talk a lot about Jesus because I love Him with all my heart," I explained, a little embarrassed by his comment.

"Then what are you doing here?" the other man asked.

"I don't really have to be here. I choose to be here because I love these people," I answered. Shaking their heads in disbelief, they asked how I could love these unlovely, smelly people.

I looked around the dark room, barely able to make out the forms of the other men. Though I couldn't see all of them, the moans and gut-wrenching sounds of their alcohol-induced vomiting made their presence obvious. "I love them because God loves them, and He has put His love in my heart. When I look at them through God's eyes, I see His children instead of people thrown onto society's junk pile."

They became quiet for a time. Unable to see their expressions, I wondered what they were thinking. Finally, one of the men asked, "Do you see yourself as having done any good?"

In complete honesty I replied, "Not often, but God has changed some of those I've ministered to on the streets, and He's given them a brand new beginning. Their hearts have been made new, and they have hope of eternal life."

They grew quiet again. Then I heard one of the men begin to cry. Putting his hand on mine, he said, "You know, I need something in my life. I look forward to weekends because I can't handle the pressures of work. Then, on the weekends, I can't handle my family. I have nothing to look forward to." Nodding in the direction of the other men in the cell, he continued, "We don't live on the streets, but we're just as messed up as they are." His despair was apparent as he quietly asked, "Can you give us the same encouragement and hope you give these guys?"

"Jesus doesn't care who you are or what you've gone through. He wants to give all men eternal life," I told him. The self-pity I'd been feeling turned into excitement as I shared the plan of salvation with these men. With tears in their eyes, they acknowledged their need for Jesus and accepted Him into their lives. Once again, a den of the Enemy had become God's holy church.

I explained to the men that their walk with God was a process. Some have had their lives changed immediately, and for some the walk was more gradual. I assured them of God's promise in His Word to give new life and told them that when we trust Him as our Savior, we have that new life. It's ours.

"I feel like a brick has been lifted from my heart," one of the men said through his tears. "What do we do next?"

Because of my arrest, and because the police wanted to teach me a lesson by keeping me locked up for a few days, I was able to spend that time teaching these men what the Bible says about living a holy life. What Satan had intended for evil, God had intended for good!

Finally our day of release came, and after a lecture from the police about the dangers of alcohol and living on the streets, we were set free. We walked out with smiles on our faces, holding hands and praying. We hugged each other good-bye and had one last prayer together as the officers looked on. I encouraged my new brothers with more scripture and told them, "It won't be easy, but the Holy Spirit will be your teacher and guide." I told them to find a Bible-believing church and to immediately begin sharing with others about the new life within them.

What a difference I felt as I left that place, compared with when I had first arrived. God always knows what He's doing, and I was thankful to be a part of His plan.

Taking It Inward

Think about the uncanny sequence of events that brought Kurt and two hurting men together in the "drunk tank" of Portland, Oregon. Of course, not knowing what God was up to, both Kurt and these men were angry and confused about being in the wrong place at the wrong time. This is the way it often seems with God! But just when we don't think we can take it anymore, God's grace and power explode on the scene, and the distressing events of our lives start to make sense.

Do you remember Joseph, the guy with the multi-colored coat from Genesis? God brought him through so many extraordinary and confusing circumstances—all so He could have the **right person** in the **right place** at the **right time**. Some highlights of Joseph's life are printed below. Some of these highlights are verses from the Bible; others just give a synopsis of events.

To help you notice the details as you read these highlights, draw a face (smiling [☺] or frowning [☹]) in each empty circle beside the verses. This face should depict how Joseph must have felt at that particular point in time.

One other thing: Underline any mention of God—and be sure to keep track of what He's doing!

Highlights of Joseph's life

○ **Genesis 37:3–5** 3 Now Israel loved Joseph more than any of his other sons, because he had been born to him in his old age; and he made a richly ornamented robe for him. 4 When his brothers saw that their father loved him more than any of them, they hated him and could not speak a kind word to him. 5 Joseph had a dream, and when he told it to his brothers, they hated him all the more.

○ **Genesis 37:23–24** 23 So when Joseph came to his brothers, they stripped him of his robe—the richly ornamented robe he was wearing— 24 and they took him and threw him into the cistern. Now the cistern was empty; there was no water in it.

○ **Genesis 37:36** ³⁶ Meanwhile, the Midianites sold Joseph in Egypt to Potiphar, one of Pharaoh's officials, the captain of the guard.

○ **Genesis 39:2–4** ² The LORD was with Joseph and he prospered, and he lived in the house of his Egyptian master. ³ When his master saw that the LORD was with him and that the LORD gave him success in everything he did, ⁴ Joseph found favor in his eyes and became his attendant. Potiphar put him in charge of his household, and he entrusted to his care everything he owned.

○ **Synopsis of Genesis 39:7–18** Potiphar's wife tried to seduce Joseph. After he resisted her many advances, she tried to frame Joseph by accusing **him** of trying to seduce **her**! And since Joseph had left his coat in her room after fleeing her advances, she possessed convincing "incriminating evidence."

○ **Genesis 39:19–21** ¹⁹ When his master heard the story his wife told him, saying, "This is how your slave treated me," he burned with anger. ²⁰ Joseph's master took him and put him in prison, the place where the king's prisoners were confined. But while Joseph was there in the prison, ²¹ the LORD was with him; he showed him kindness and granted him favor in the eyes of the prison warden.

○ **Genesis 41:15–16** ¹⁵ Pharaoh said to Joseph, "I had a dream, and no one can interpret it. But I have heard it said of you that when you hear a dream you can interpret it." ¹⁶ "I cannot do it," Joseph replied to Pharaoh, "but God will give Pharaoh the answer he desires."

○ **Synopsis of Genesis 41:17–38** Joseph's interpretation of Pharaoh's dream revealed that God would soon bring seven years of abundant harvest, followed by seven years of famine. Joseph instructed Pharaoh on how to take advantage of this great harvest in order to be prepared for the famine.

○ **Genesis 41:39–41** ³⁹ Then Pharaoh said to Joseph, "Since God has made all this known to you, there is no one so discerning and wise as you. ⁴⁰ You shall be in charge of my palace, and all my people are to submit to your orders. Only with respect to the throne will I be greater than you." ⁴¹ So Pharaoh said to Joseph, "I hereby put you in charge of the whole land of Egypt."

○ **Synopsis of Genesis 42:1–7** Because Joseph had successfully predicted the coming famine, Egypt was prepared and became the only source of food for the entire region. So Joseph's brothers came to Egypt to buy food for their families. Since Pharaoh had appointed Joseph to be the distributor of food, Joseph's office was the first stop for his brothers.

○ **Genesis 42:8** ⁸ Although Joseph recognized his brothers, they did not recognize him.

○ **Genesis 45:1–3** ¹ Then Joseph could no longer control himself before all his attendants, and he cried out, "Have everyone leave my presence!" So there was no one with Joseph when he made himself known to his brothers. ² And he wept so loudly that the Egyptians heard him, and Pharaoh's household heard about it. ³ Joseph said to his brothers, "I am Joseph! Is my father still living?" But his brothers were not able to answer him, because they were terrified at his presence.

○ **Genesis 50:18–20** ¹⁸ His brothers then came and threw themselves down before him. "We are your slaves," they said. ¹⁹ But Joseph said to them, "Don't be afraid. Am I in the place of God? ²⁰ You intended to harm me, but God intended it for good to accomplish what is now being done, the saving of many lives.

Joseph's family was saved. All of Egypt was preserved. And God used these events to begin growing the mighty nation of Israel. Now count up your "faces." How many smiley faces do you have? _____ How about the frowning faces? _____

Look back at Genesis 39:19–21. What do you notice about Joseph's circumstances and the presence of the Lord?

FRI_{Day} 5

Do you think Joseph—at this point in his story—had good reason to ask "Why me?" How about you? What's happening in your life that's causing you to ask "Why me?" Write something in the space below, and be specific!

Now, reread Genesis 50:20 and answer a couple of questions:

      1. How does this verse relate to Kurt's experience of being arrested?

      2. How can this verse apply to the "Why me?" circumstances in your life?

At any point in Kurt's or Joseph's experiences, they could have lashed out at God—and in doing so, each might have changed the way his story ended. Joseph's story, which ended on a miraculously high note, had a lot of "frowning face" situations. Same with Kurt. And probably with you, too.

When we're in the middle of a "Why me?" situation, we often feel distant from God. Yet all the while, God is orchestrating events that will bring results far greater than we can imagine. Take a moment to read the verses below. Then journal any thoughts that come to mind.

Ephesians 3:13–21 (linger on verse 20!)   **James 1:1–4**

Seal the Deal

Write out a short prayer that: 1) acknowledges to God any difficulty you're facing right now; 2) tells God how you're going to look for Him to use that difficulty for His work; and 3) asks Him to show you the hurting people in the "jail cell" with you, who might be able to use your help!

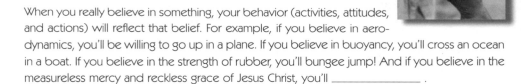

Do Day

Do not merely listen to the word, and so deceive yourselves. **Do what it says.**

—James 1:22 (emphasis added)

When you really believe in something, your behavior (activities, attitudes, and actions) will reflect that belief. For example, if you believe in aerodynamics, you'll be willing to go up in a plane. If you believe in buoyancy, you'll cross an ocean in a boat. If you believe in the strength of rubber, you'll bungee jump! And if you believe in the measureless mercy and reckless grace of Jesus Christ, you'll _____ .

We want to help you fill in that blank. That's why we've designated each Saturday as a "Do Day" —to help you share Jesus' mercy with the people around you. Many of the activities suggested are related to the stories and Bible studies you've completed each week. We're not expecting you to do all the activities—just try one or two and allow God to speak to you through the activities you choose.

Done	Ministry Activity
☐	Today, love somebody "to the Max" (see Day 3 for an explanation of that phrase). Anonymously give a week's worth of your wages to a friend in financial distress.
☐	Sign up to personally sponsor a child through a ministry like Compassion International or another Christian child development ministry. Look for their advertisements in most Christian magazines or find them on the web.
☐	Do an act of brotherly love for someone you listed in Day 4's "Seal the Deal"— someone who you suspect could be lonely.
☐	Call some friends and take a "new kid in town" shopping or to a ball game.
☐	Grab a friend and fix a meal for a widow/widower.

Worship

And let us consider how we may **spur one another on** toward love and good deeds. **Let us not give up meeting together**, as some are in the habit of doing, but let us **encourage one another**—and all the more as you see the Day approaching.
—Hebrews 10:24–25 (emphasis added)

A note from Kurt: "I never take a Sunday to do ministry on the streets. I want to worship with God's people in God's house."

Dedicate this day to listening to God. He may be trying to get your attention through the stories and scriptures you've read this week. Today, give Him time to get through to you. Take this book to church, and use these pages for taking notes on your worship and learning experiences.

Sunday School

Subject:

Bible passages referred to:

What are at least two things you can begin applying **today** from this lesson?

Worship

Write a prayer (perhaps during the offering time or just before the service begins) that expresses your gratitude for His mercy and grace.

SUN_{Day} 7

Sermon

Subject/Title:

Scripture text:

Key points:

Cool thoughts or observations:

What did God say to you through this sermon?

What is He asking you to change?

Connections

How did God weave together your experiences of the week with your worship and learning today? Take a moment to write down any connections in the space below.

Week 2

Day 8   The Coat
Day 9   Friends
Day 10   The Prostitute
Day 11   Satan's Pursuit
Day 12   Sun Bear
Day 13   Do Day
Day 14   Worship

The Coat

Christmas at my house was always so exciting. The house would be decorated from floor to rafter, the tree surrounded by brightly wrapped packages, some with my name on them. I always assumed the gifts were from both my parents, but years later I realized that my dad had had nothing to do with the gift planning, buying, or wrapping. Mom had done it all.

I really didn't know my dad. He worked all the time, and his job frequently took him out of town. He stayed very uninvolved in my life, and I was never really sure how he felt about me. Eventually my mom and dad were divorced, causing even more distance between us. But, I longed to know my dad. I longed to understand who he really was and to feel his love.

It was the Christmas break of my freshman year at college, and I went home to celebrate the holidays with my family. First I visited my mom's house to enjoy eating great food and opening gifts. Then I left to visit my dad. He greeted me at the door with a big box with my name on it. I couldn't believe it! My dad had actually gone out and purchased a gift for me all by himself. I was deeply moved that he would do this for me, and for the first time ever, I felt his concern for me.

"I was worried about you being in Portland this winter without a warm coat, so I got you one," he explained as I tore open the box. Inside, I found a beautiful fur-lined coat. It was perfect! How could he have known how badly I needed this coat? I had never mentioned my work on the streets to him. Joy and gratitude overwhelmed me, and I gave my dad a big hug to show my appreciation.

MON Day 8

Visiting my family had been so special that year, and I went back to school feeling warm and loved. Soon, however, I was back on the cold streets of Portland, ministering to the homeless there. As the days and nights grew colder, I became even more grateful for my dad's gift of the fur-lined coat.

Walking along the cracked sidewalk one day, I saw a man wearing a thin, sleeveless jacket. It was obvious he was very cold, and the skin on his arms was red from exposure.

"What can I do for this man?" I asked God.

"Give him your coat."

The thought stopped me in my tracks. Surely God didn't expect me to give this undeserving street bum the only thing my dad had ever given me in my entire life. My benevolence instantly turned to resentment. I argued, "But he doesn't deserve this coat!" How could God expect me to give away something so precious to me?

"My Son gave His life for you, and you didn't deserve that either." I could clearly hear God speaking, and I was aware that His Son was precious to Him, too. There was no denying it. To make matters even worse, I had just been studying the book of Acts, where I learned that the believers sold their possessions and gave to anyone in need. At the time I read it, I thought it was a great concept and very admirable. Now I was being required to practice what the Bible taught—and I wasn't so enthusiastic about it!

I'd like to say I had perfect peace as I touched the man's arm to get his attention, but that would be a lie. "I was admiring your jacket," I told him. "I was hoping you'd let me try it on."

He looked at me with curiosity, as if to say, "This old thing?" I took off my warm, precious coat, handed it to him, and slipped on the ripped, filthy jacket the man had been wearing.

"This is perfect. Just what I wanted," I told him. "Will you trade me?"

The man looked at me like I was crazy. "Okay, uh, sure," he answered. As he put on the new coat he asked, "Is this some kind of a joke?"

"No," I answered. "The Jesus in me wants you to have it. Merry Christmas."

I turned to walk away, hoping the man hadn't noticed I was choking back tears. I found the nearest light post and leaned against it as my heart broke in two. Now I could no longer hold back the tears. A complete stranger was wearing the special coat my dad had intended for me.

I returned to my dorm room that night, wet and cold in the useless, worn-out jacket I had traded for. "Sometimes I really don't understand," I thought as I walked sadly down the dark hallway toward my room.

Outside my door was a small brown paper bag with my name on it. "That's strange," I thought. I opened the bag and looked inside. There, to my surprise, was a stack of dollar bills neatly secured with a rubber band. As I removed the rubber band, a note fell out that said, "To Kurt." The bag had apparently been sitting there for two weeks. My roommates must have kept stepping over it, thinking it was some old sack lunch I'd left behind.

Now I could buy a new coat! It could never replace the one my dad had given me, but at least I would be warm. Surely, this was a gift from God.

I convinced my roommate to drive me into town to go shopping. We went from store to store, finding coats that were either too big, too small, or too expensive. Eventually my roommate grew tired of running all over town, so he left me to shop by myself.

Finally I saw it—the perfect coat, there in the store window. I hurried into the store, found the coat, and read the price tag. There was no way I could ever hope to afford that coat.

As I stood there in my disappointment, the sales clerk walked up. "Do you need any help?" she asked.

"No, I don't have enough money for this coat anyway."

She didn't seem to be listening as she took the coat off the hanger and helped me put it on. "It fits you perfectly," she said.

The coat did fit perfectly, and I loved it. "God, why couldn't You have given me enough money to pay for this? Why didn't You help me find one that fit *and* that I could afford?" My whining was even getting on *my* nerves!

The sales clerk noticed my disappointment and told me to wait there for her, she would be right back. While she was gone I counted the money one more time to see if perhaps God had multiplied it while I wasn't looking. He hadn't.

"How much money do you have?" the clerk asked when she returned. I handed her the brown paper bag, and she counted each dollar bill. "This is exactly enough. The coat is yours."

"Praise God!" I blurted out, a little embarrassed.

"Amen," she replied as she made her way to the cash register. I thanked her, and she handed me the receipt for my brand new coat.

As I walked away from that store, I knew beyond a shadow of a doubt that not only did my earthly father love me and care about my needs, my heavenly Father did as well.

Taking It Inward

Kurt's offer to trade his fur-lined coat for a sleeveless, worn-out jacket seems extraordinary to us. But it shouldn't. This sort of thing should be common with God's people. All through the Bible, God said that if we lock our minds and hearts on **His** world, we'll be able to loosen our grip on the things of **our** world.

Jesus had a lot to say about this when He walked about our world. Luke 12 contains one of His most powerful teachings on how and why we should let God determine our priorities. Don't miss this! As you read the verses below, write in the space provided your responses to the questions in the right column.

Luke 12:22–40

²² Then Jesus said to his disciples: "Therefore I tell you, do not worry about your life, what you will eat; or about your body, what you will wear. ²³ Life is more than food, and the body more than clothes. ²⁴ Consider the ravens: They do not sow or reap, they have no storeroom or barn; yet God feeds them. And how much more valuable you are than birds! ²⁵ Who of you by worrying can add a single hour to his life ? ²⁶ Since you cannot do this very little thing, why do you worry about the rest? ²⁷ "Consider how the lilies grow. They do not labor or spin. Yet I tell you, not even Solomon in all his splendor was dressed like one of these. ²⁸ If that is how God clothes the grass of the field, which is here today, and tomorrow is thrown into the fire, how much more will he clothe you, O you of little faith!

What four things did Jesus tell his disciples (and us!) **not** to worry about?

1.

2.

3.

4.

Now make a list of everything you see that God wants to do for us.

Mercy Beyond Measure – **The Coat**

29 And do not set your heart on what you will eat or drink; do not worry about it. 30 For the pagan world runs after all such things, and your Father knows that you need them. 31 But seek his kingdom, and these things will be given to you as well. 32 "Do not be afraid, little flock, for your Father has been pleased to give you the kingdom. 33 Sell your possessions and give to the poor. Provide purses for yourselves that will not wear out, a treasure in heaven that will not be exhausted, where no thief comes near and no moth destroys. 34 For where your treasure is, there your heart will be also.

35 "Be dressed ready for service and keep your lamps burning, 36 like men waiting for their master to return from a wedding banquet, so that when he comes and knocks they can immediately open the door for him. 37 It will be good for those servants whose master finds them watching when he comes. I tell you the truth, he will dress himself to serve, will have them recline at the table and will come and wait on them. 38 It will be good for those servants whose master finds them ready, even if he comes in the second or third watch of the night. 39 But understand this: If the owner of the house had known at what hour the thief was coming, he would not have let his house be broken into. 40 You also must be ready, because the Son of Man will come at an hour when you do not expect him."

What did Jesus tell His disciples to do regarding the people around them?

What future event did Jesus tie in with His teaching on material things?

In this passage Jesus teaches us about the type of behavior and the kind of heart He wants us to have until He returns. If you were to do what Jesus said—not worry about your life, let God sweat the details, and seek God's kingdom before anything else—what would change in your life? Chew on that one for a minute. Then list two or three changes you can make.

Did you notice how Kurt was rewarded for his obedience? God's promises are true! Remember what Jesus said in one of the verses you just read:

Luke 12:28

> 28 If that is how God clothes the grass of the field, which is here today, and tomorrow is thrown into the fire, how much more will he clothe you, O you of little faith!

Try God out on this next promise. He actually told us we could test Him in this area!

Malachi 3:10

> 10 "Bring the whole tithe into the storehouse, that there may be food in my house. Test me in this," says the LORD Almighty, "and see if I will not throw open the floodgates of heaven and pour out so much blessing that you will not have room enough for it."

Seal the Deal

Jesus raised the stakes when He said, "O you of little faith." The size of our faith is directly related to our ability to let go of the things of our world—and trust Him to clothe us with things from **His** world. Here are some ways to take some "baby steps" toward loosening your grip on this world, while locking in on God's world:

1. Go through your closet and look for items you can take to a thrift store. Make sure the items are good and wearable. (Remember Kurt's coat!)

MON_{Day} 8

2. Commit to giving the Lord 10 percent of **any** income (baby sitting, allowance, etc.) for the next four weeks as a start. If you already do that, try upping it to 15 percent.

3. Collect a few friends for a group grocery store run. Take the groceries to a mission, food pantry, or homeless shelter in your community.

Friends

Inner cities are notorious for having large homosexual populations. Some of the more aggressive and dangerous homosexuals hang out in certain hotels and sit at the windows to watch and choose their victims. If they spot someone who attracts them, they will begin to stalk them, waiting for the right moment to attack and sexually assault. Some of the more depraved will even roam the streets looking for drunks who have passed out somewhere and rape them while they sleep. Some of these drunks never wake up again, because the homosexual men will brutally murder them in their sleep. This is why most homeless men have a buddy whom they look out for and who looks out for them at all times.

It was 3:00 A.M., and I was standing on the corner talking with a few of the bums. Suddenly a truck drove up and stopped in the middle of the street. Two homosexual men jumped out. One man grabbed my arms and the other grabbed my legs. They had obviously been watching me and had decided I was their victim for that night. Right in front of everyone they tried to put me in their truck and take me away! It happened so fast that I didn't have time to defend myself. One of the bums who had been standing on the corner with me began fighting with the two men, trying to get me free. One of the homosexuals punched him, knocking him to the ground. Several more of my street friends jumped in the middle of the fight to save me from certain rape and possibly even death. Time and again they were knocked to the ground, but each time they'd get up swinging.

Finally one of the bums yelled, "Kurt's getting hurt! We need help!"

What happened next was astonishing. Bums came out of buildings and climbed out of garbage bins. They ran out of the alleys. Every imaginable hiding place delivered up more of my street friends. Soon the truck was surrounded by a gang of derelicts determined to do whatever it took to set me free. They physically overpowered the two men. Seeing that they were outnumbered and had no chance of getting me into the truck, they dropped me on the ground, striking my head on the hood of the truck.

There I sat in the middle of the street, rubbing my sore head, completely stunned by what had just taken place. I couldn't believe all of the men who'd come out of the shadows to defend me. It was then that I realized how many friends I had made over the weeks and months I had lived on the streets.

Soon the police came, and we all ended up in the drunk tank. As we sat together in the jail cell, I was touched by the concern my friends showered on me. I prayed, "Lord, what a beautiful feeling to be cared for by other people. The only thing these men have to give away is love, and they have given it to me." I couldn't help but feel that they were trying to give back some of what I had given them. I was touched. I realized they had helped me because they cherished our friendship.

What a comfort to be ministered to by those to whom I had ministered.

Taking It Inward

Think for a minute of all the encouragers in your life. Perhaps this includes a youth pastor, a volunteer youth worker, a family member, or a friend who comforts and helps you in your struggles. Write the names of these people in the space below.

My Encouragers

Here's the question: Would Kurt have survived this incident without the help of his friends? Probably not. What a great way (though Kurt didn't think so at the time) for the Lord to show us how vital it is for us to help our friends.

It's nearly impossible to minister—or even live!—without some form of encouragement or affirmation once in awhile. But God never intended for people to do work of any kind alone. In fact, the one thing God said was "not good" in all of creation was the fact that Adam was working solo. So God made a "suitable helper" for him. We're all in need of "suitable helpers"—friends (and perhaps someday a husband or a wife) who will come alongside us in the work we do.

Read the passages below as if your life depended on them—because it does! These verses are taken from letters written to Christians experiencing intense religious persecution. The instructions God gives in these passages are intended to preserve your life in a world that's trying to destroy you! So to be sure you don't miss anything, underline every instruction regarding **how** we're to help those around us. Also look for words like "one another," "each other," "those," and "them," and mark these in a unique way.

1 Thessalonians 5:11–14

[11] Therefore encourage one another and build each other up, just as in fact you are doing. [12] Now we ask you, brothers, to respect those who work hard among you, who are over you in the Lord and who admonish you. [13] Hold them in the highest regard in love because of their work. Live in peace with each other. [14] And we urge you, brothers, warn those who are idle, encourage the timid, help the weak, be patient with everyone.

Hebrews 3:12–19

[12] See to it, brothers, that none of you has a sinful, unbelieving heart that turns away from the living God. [13] But encourage one another daily, as long as it is called Today, so that none of you may be hardened by sin's deceitfulness. [14] We have come to share in Christ if we hold firmly till the end the confidence we had at first. [15] As has just been said: "Today, if you hear his voice, do not harden your hearts as you did in the rebellion." [16] Who were they who heard and rebelled? Were they not all those Moses led out of Egypt? [17] And with whom was he angry for forty years? Was it not with those who sinned, whose bodies fell in the desert? [18] And to whom did God swear that they would never enter his rest if not to those who disobeyed? [19] So we see that they were not able to enter, because of their unbelief.

TUE_{Day} 9

TUE_{Day} 9

TUEDay 9

TUE Day 9

Hebrews 10:23-25

> 23 Let us hold unswervingly to the hope we profess, for he who promised is faithful. 24 And let us consider how we may spur one another on toward love and good deeds. 25 Let us not give up meeting together, as some are in the habit of doing, but let us encourage one another—and all the more as you see the Day approaching.

Look back at everything you've underlined, and take a minute to list below everything we're to do **with** and **for** the people around us.

Helping Those Around Us

Seal the Deal

Now do this: Match each name from your "encouragers" list with an instruction from the list you just made. Then **do the instruction**! Send a note, place a call, or make a visit that encourages, builds up, and spurs someone toward love. But don't make this a one-time deal! Make it a lifestyle. It took a crisis for Kurt to experience the support and protection of his friends. Don't let that be the case with the people God has put in your life to minister to you. Encouragement really is a matter of survival!

The Prostitute

It was late, but I wasn't sleepy. It was my habit on the streets to sleep during the day and stay awake at night. It was much safer that way. Besides, nighttime was when the bums seemed to come to life and when I got my best opportunities to share Jesus.

Feeling around in my pocket for the two quarters I had panhandled for earlier that evening, I set out for a cup of coffee.

"Do you have a cigarette?" a woman's voice asked from the shadows.

"No, they make me gag," I answered. I squinted into the darkness to see who had spoken to me.

"My name is Kim," she laughed. "What's yours?"

I told her it was Kurt, and we started talking as we walked.

"Do you want to go to bed with me?" Her question came out of nowhere. I stood there completely speechless and dumbfounded. If she could have seen my face more clearly, I'm sure she would have seen me blush.

Kim broke the awkward silence. "The work is slow tonight," she said. "It won't cost you anything. I mean, you know, for anything you want."

"W-W-W-Walk with me awhile," I stuttered, trying desperately to regain my composure. I wanted very much to talk to her about her life, but I didn't have a clue how to start. I asked the obvious: "Are you a prostitute?"

"Well, I prefer to be called a lady of the night." She smiled shyly as she said this, and I sensed an openness about her. She seemed anxious to talk to someone. I hoped she would be open to hearing about Jesus.

We continued to walk and found that we enjoyed talking to one another. I asked her some very direct questions about her life of prostitution. She, in turn, didn't hesitate to ask me about my stuttering and my life. An honesty and trust developed between us as we talked, and in less than an hour we had shared quite a lot about ourselves.

I learned that Kim had been a prostitute since she was a child. Her mother lived on the streets, and she didn't see any other option but to do as her mother had done to survive. So, night after night, she would sell herself on the streets for money or a warm place to stay.

"It's really not that bad a life," she insisted, but we both knew it was a lie.

"Kim, do you want to get off the streets?" My question agitated her.

"That's impossible!" she replied hotly.

"You know, Kim, Jesus can give you new life within—and He can make it possible for a new life on the outside, too."

She looked at me so intently and listened to my words as if her life depended on it. I could see hope in her eyes that what I said was true. Maybe there really was a way out of her horrible existence. Soon a tear ran down her cheek.

"Here," I said. "Let's sit down. Tell me what you're feeling."

We sat down against the cold brick wall of a building, and Kim began to pour out her heart. She told me how desperately she wished her life could be different. Deep emotion swept over her as she struggled for words that would adequately express her feelings.

"I want a new life. I want to feel clean on the inside, not guilty and dirty. Maybe I could have a better life. I want to hope for that." Her words were urgent and sincere. "If I'm going to change, I've got to get off these streets!" After a tentative pause she added, "And I want to marry Tom."

"Who's Tom?" I asked. I was surprised by the sudden turn in our conversation.

"There's a bank where I deposit the money I make each night. Tom is a teller there. I only see him at the bank and when he takes me to lunch. I've been seeing him this way for over two years." Tears welled up in her eyes again. "He asked me to marry him once when we were at lunch. I told him no. How could I marry him when he doesn't even know who or what I am? I've lied to him about where I live, what I do—everything." Sobs racked her body now as she choked out her pain and disappointment. "But I did tell him I want a family someday—and a nice home. It would be so different than...than this!" She looked with disgust up and down the dismal street.

I had asked a simple question and was blown away by this amazing confession. Kim and I talked all night about what it would be like to find new life in Christ. As her tears flowed, she asked Jesus into her heart, holding tight to the hope of becoming a new creation.

The sunrise that morning seemed to symbolize Kim's new life and relationship with Christ. The question looming before us this bright new day was what to do about Tom. Feeling sure that God would work this out for Kim, I told her, "Concentrate and pray with me. Ask God to guide your new life, whether it's with Tom or not."

We sat silently for a time, and Kim suddenly announced, "I'll call Tom and tell him everything." She pulled his number out of her purse as we hurried to the nearest phone booth. I dug into my pocket for one of my two quarters. Her hands shook as she deposited it into the pay phone. Suddenly she shoved Tom's phone number at me and said, "You talk to him. I'm too scared, and I'll start to cry again."

Kim had no idea what she was asking. I stuttered badly enough talking face to face, and it was always much worse over the telephone.

Our call woke Tom up that Saturday morning, and he answered with a groggy, "Hello." Before I could stutter through the word "Hi," he hung up, thinking it was a prank call. I dug into my pocket again and retrieved my last quarter. I dropped the quarter into the phone and dialed the number, determined to make it through the introduction before he hung up on me. This time I managed to say, "You don't know me—" before he slammed the phone in my ear.

It was Kim's turn to dig for a quarter. This was our last shot. As soon as Tom picked up the phone I shouted, "Tom, don't hang up!" He demanded to know who I was and why I was calling so early in the morning. When I told him I was with Kim, his tone changed from irritation to concern. Praying that God would supply the right words, I told him that Kim was living on the streets. I explained that I'd met her the night before and had led her to accept Jesus Christ as her Savior. Then I handed the phone to a very apprehensive Kim.

I stood by, offering my prayerful support as she struggled through the truth about her life on the streets and about the prostitution. She said she would understand if he never wanted to see her again. Several times I heard her tell him she loved him and that her life had truly been changed.

"Tom's coming," Kim said anxiously as she hung up the phone. "He said not to leave. I'm not sure he believes me." We prayed and put the matter in God's able hands. There was nothing else to do but sit and wait.

It seemed like hours before Tom arrived. Kim was dressed in her "work" clothes and wondered aloud what Tom would think when he saw her that way. I couldn't imagine what he would think. I just continued to pray.

Finally, Tom pulled up across the street from where we sat. "That's him," Kim said nervously. She hugged me good-bye. "Thank you, Kurt," she said as she hurried across the street.

Tom stood motionless for a long time as Kim told him the truth about her life. Then he gently reached out and took her hand in his. They got into his car and drove away, and it seemed to me as if a cloud of angels followed behind. I prayed for them as I watched them leave, thanking God for Kim's new life on the inside and the outside. Who but God could perform such an amazing miracle of love?

Taking It Inward

It's so easy to underestimate the power of the gospel. The message of Jesus Christ can actually transform you! It can give you a clean break from your past—your former habits, past mistakes, and wrong decisions—no questions asked! Yet people still wallow in the deception that they're not clean enough for God. All the while God is eagerly, **desperately** waiting for them to accept the fact that He can clean them up!

Kim was convinced that her past had left her no other option but a life on the streets; she had even believed the lie that a life of prostitution wasn't that bad a life! But miracles happen when the dirt of the world meets the Light of the world. In John 8, a group of pious religious leaders threw a despised, dirty woman at the feet of pure, sinless Jesus. Let's see what happened when this woman encountered the Light—two thousand years before Kim did. As you read the passage below, mark every mention of the woman with a female stick figure [🧍].

John 8:3–11

3 The teachers of the law and the Pharisees brought in a woman caught in adultery. They made her stand before the group 4 and said to Jesus, "Teacher, this woman was caught in the act of adultery. 5 In the Law Moses commanded us to stone such women. Now what do you say?" 6 They were using this question as a trap, in order to have a basis for accusing him. But Jesus bent down and started to write on the ground with his finger.

WED_{Day} 10

> ⁷ When they kept on questioning him, he straightened up and said to them, "If any one of you is without sin, let him be the first to throw a stone at her." ⁸ Again he stooped down and wrote on the ground. ⁹ At this, those who heard began to go away one at a time, the older ones first, until only Jesus was left, with the woman still standing there. ¹⁰ Jesus straightened up and asked her, "Woman, where are they? Has no one condemned you?" ¹¹ "No one, sir," she said. "Then neither do I condemn you," Jesus declared. "Go now and leave your life of sin."

With a single sentence, Jesus released the woman from her past and gave her hope for the future. That's transformational power!

Two words in Scripture illustrate the power of the gospel better than any other—**justified** and **transformed**. In fact, every time you see the word **justified** in the Bible, you should substitute it with the phrase "just as if I'd never sinned." That's exactly what the word means—and it's an offer only Jesus Christ can make!

When you see the word **transformed**, think of the word **metamorphosis**. Remember that word from science? It's used to describe a caterpillar metamorphosing into a butterfly. **Metamorphose** is the Greek word (Greek being the original language of the New Testament) that we translate **transformed**. That's the power of the gospel; it can erase your mistakes—as if they've never happened—and can change you into someone entirely new! For most of us, that's good news!

Now that you understand these words, take a moment to see what the Bible says about being **justified** and **transformed**.

Justified—Just As If I'd Never Sinned
As you read the verses below, journal beneath the references everything you learn about being justified. Try to find out **who** can be justified, **how** we are justified, and **who** or **what** does the justifying.

Romans 3:21–26   **Romans 5:1–9**   **Titus 3:3–7**

Transformed—Metamorphosis

Check out these verses too, and write down every detail you learn about transformation. As you read, ask yourself questions like: **What are we being transformed into? Who or what is doing the transforming? What's the result of this transformation?**

2 Corinthians 3:17–18   **Romans 12:1–2**

Seal the Deal

What mistakes or regrets would you like to be free from? Do you now see that you can be free from your past **today**? All the dirt and the guilt can be swept away—made just as if it never happened. The question is: Do you want this? If so, write a bold "YES" in the box below. Then call a trusted Christian friend to help you get started with your new life.

One more thing: Is there anyone in your life who might be like Kim? Do you have a friend who feels haunted by past mistakes and bad decisions? Write his or her name in the space below. Then begin praying that the darkness of this friend's life will be overcome by the Light of the world—just like it was with Kim and the adulterous woman in John 8. Pray, too, that God will reveal how you might play a role in leading this person to a life-changing encounter with Jesus.

After you've prayed, begin listening. Listen for your friend to say something like what Kim said to Kurt: "I want a new life. I want to feel clean on the inside, not guilty and dirty." Be ready to respond with the good news of Jesus Christ.

Satan's Pursuit

L ife on the streets is one of contrasts, and this particular day was no exception. Two men had just become children of the King, owners of castles in heaven, equal to all who are in the Lord. I felt warm in spite of the cold wind as I reflected on the great things God had done.

Suddenly, out of nowhere, I heard someone shout, "You ——— ——— Christian!" I turned to see who was yelling the obscenities, but all I saw was a group of men sitting against a building. They were huddled so close together that it was impossible to tell who was yelling at me. I said a prayer as the insults and obscenities continued to fly in my direction, knowing that God loved this man, whoever he was, and that I needed to show him that love.

Suddenly, I saw him. He had a crowbar in his hand and was coming toward me, his eyes blazing with brutal intent. I ducked just in time to hear the *whoosh* of the bar as it passed dangerously close to my skull. Looking up from my crouched position, I saw the man swing again. Jumping back barely in time, I took off running, with the crazed attacker close at my heels.

I ran track in high school and was thankful for what endurance I still had. But no matter how hard I ran, I could not shake this man. He seemed to possess unusual strength and stamina. I ran for several blocks, thinking he would soon wear out, but he continued hot on my heels, screaming blasphemies about my Lord. As I ran and prayed, in the midst of this terrible threat, great peace came over me. I remember asking God, "Why, on such a victorious day, would I be chased by a crazed man wanting to kill me?" Immediately the scriptures where Paul talked about our weapons of spiritual warfare came to mind, and I began to understand what was happening. *Satan was mad!*

The few quick glimpses I'd gotten of the man told me I had never met him before. I knew it wasn't humanly possible for him to have known of the events of that day, yet I heard him yelling, "Jesus is not Lord! You'd better stop telling lies that make men believe. Satan will get back at those men today!" The realization of what was occurring began to sink in. My breath became short as I realized I was involved in something much too big to handle alone. I needed God's help, and quickly.

It was getting late as I ducked into old buildings and alleys, still trying to lose my pursuer, but he persisted. I had lived in these streets on and off for more than a year, so I knew even the most obscure routes and hiding places, and I headed for one of them now. I ran toward a familiar bar at the end of an alley.

I bolted through the front door, my eyes darting around for a place to hide. I spotted an empty bar stool in the middle of a group of men and figured I would blend in there. At first the men were startled by my sudden and disheveled appearance, so I tried to make small talk so I would fit in. Finally, I was safe.

Still keeping an apprehensive eye on the door, I soon relaxed, relieved that I had lost this man so intent on killing me. I began to listen to the conversations going on around me and was once again surprised by the number of times I heard men talking about God. As I sat there, relaxing more as the minutes passed, I heard one man say, "What the mission preacher said about God was a lie. God is dead."

"But that's not true," I told the man. I talked to Him only fifteen minutes ago, and believe me, I know He is alive." All eyes turned in my direction, and I found myself barraged by questions. The bartender shook his head in disbelief that these conversations were going on in his bar. I loved it!

After several hours and a lot of good conversation, I stood to tell my new friends good-bye. I assured them I'd be praying for them and that my prayer would be for them to know God personally and intimately.

I stepped into the street, taking a deep breath to clear my head of the smell of smoke and stale alcohol. That's when my quiet thoughts were shattered by the same man screaming, "Christian, I'm going to find you and kill you!" I had planned to spend the night on the streets, but I hopped on the first bus heading toward campus instead!

As the bus took me from the brutality and desperation of the streets back to my comfortable dorm room and warm bed, it occurred to me that Satan too was very much alive. There is a battle being fought that we can't see, and though it rages on, the war has been won. Christ has defeated the Enemy and is the Victor. Praise God, I'm on His side!

Taking It Inward

When you're on a spiritual mountaintop, you should know one thing: Satan is nearby, trying to knock you off! You can count on it—in fact, you'd better expect it. The entire Bible—Genesis to Revelation—is a record of Satan's work to destroy us and God's work to rescue us. God has given us everything we need to be rescued and protected. But it's up to us to trust God's Word.

Let's drop in on three instances in scripture where we see both the certainty of Satan's work and the assurance of God's protection.

The Certainty of Satan's Pursuit While on the Mountaintop

As you read these verses, underline what happened to Jesus just before the Devil came to tempt Him. Draw a clock [🕐] at the point where Satan made his appearance.

Matthew 3:16–4:1

16 As soon as Jesus was baptized, he went up out of the water. At that moment heaven was opened, and he saw the Spirit of God descending like a dove and lighting on him.

17 And a voice from heaven said, "This is my Son, whom I love; with him I am well pleased."

4:1 Then Jesus was led by the Spirit into the desert to be tempted by the devil.

THU~Day~ 11

How would you describe Jesus' spiritual high?

☐   so-so
☐   pretty cool
☐   awesome—God was there!

How would you describe Satan's timing after Jesus' spiritual high?

☐   He took his time, letting Jesus enjoy His spiritual experience.
☐   He seemed in no particular hurry.
☐   His timing may have been calculated.
☐   He jumped on Jesus the first chance he got.

The Certainty of Satan's Pursuit and the Promise of Rescue

As you read the next passage, draw a pitchfork [🔱] over anything Jesus says about the trouble we will have. Draw a cloud [☁] around anything that gives you hope.

John 16:32–33 (Jesus is speaking to His disciples)

> 32 "But a time is coming, and has come, when you will be scattered, each to his own home. You will leave me all alone. Yet I am not alone, for my Father is with me. 33 "I have told you these things, so that in me you may have peace. In this world you will have trouble. But take heart! I have overcome the world."

Now underline the two-word phrase Jesus used to describe the certainty of trouble coming our way. Think about that phrase for a second. If it's certain we "will have" trouble, how does Jesus want us to respond to it?

Why are we able to respond that way?

The Certainty of Satan's Pursuit and the Promise of Protection

After you read the passage below, list what we **are** and **are not** wrestling against.

Are Wrestling Against	Are Not Wrestling Against
1.	1.
2.	2.
3.	
4.	

Ephesians 6:10–12

> [10] Finally, be strong in the Lord and in his mighty power. [11] Put on the full armor of God so that you can take your stand against the devil's schemes. [12] For our struggle is not against flesh and blood, but against the rulers, against the authorities, against the powers of this dark world and against the spiritual forces of evil in the heavenly realms.

Because our battle is against spiritual hosts and rulers, we need spiritual equipment! Paul, the author of Ephesians, describes this equipment in the passage on the next page. As you read it, write in the chart each piece of armor and what it represents spiritually. Don't worry about the third column for now.

Ephesians 6:13–20	Armor Piece	What It Represents	To Do
¹³ Therefore put on the full armor of God, so that when the day of evil comes, you may be able to stand your ground, and after you have done everything, to stand. ¹⁴ Stand firm then, with the belt of truth buckled around your waist, with the breastplate of righteousness in place, ¹⁵ and with your feet fitted with the readiness that comes from the gospel of peace. ¹⁶ In addition to all this, take up the shield of faith, with which you can extinguish all the flaming arrows of the evil one. ¹⁷ Take the helmet of salvation and the sword of the Spirit, which is the word of God. ¹⁸ And pray in the Spirit on all occasions with all kinds of prayers and requests. With this in mind, be alert and always keep on praying for all the saints. ¹⁹ Pray also for me, that whenever I open my mouth, words may be given me so that I will fearlessly make known the mystery of the gospel, ²⁰ for which I am an ambassador in chains. Pray that I may declare it fearlessly, as I should.			

Does your life seem to be battle-free at the moment? If so, ponder these questions:

1. What are your temptations? This is the first place a battle can begin. Satan's pursuit is seldom as visible as it was with Kurt, but it's just as dangerous. Make a list below of the things that tempt you (write in code if you need to)—this will be a start point in identifying your battles.

2. Is your life being used to spread the gospel or expand the kingdom of God? If not, maybe Satan has already assessed you as ineffective, and you pose no threat to him. Is that really the way you want it? Think seriously about this.

Seal the Deal

Whether you're currently battle-free or engaged in a battle, if you're a Christian, you **are** fighting a spiritual war!

Look at the chart you completed earlier. Beside each piece of armor, write something you can do to "put on" or strengthen that particular piece. For example, beside "The Sword— The Word of God" you might write: **1. Develop a personal Bible study plan. 2. Get into a small book of the Bible—own it for a week! 3. Read a one-chapter book (like Jude or Philemon) in one sitting.**

For the next seven days, as soon as you get out of bed in the morning, put on your armor. Pray over each piece of armor as you visualize putting it on. As you saw in Kurt's story and in scripture, Satan is constantly on the attack. Don't get caught without your armor on.

Sun Bear

Why is it that people allow alcohol to rob them of everyone and everything that's important to them? Alcohol distorts, lies, and steals—yet millions fall victim to it.

Sun Bear was a victim of this kind of distortion when he and I first bumped into each other. He was walking out of a bar as I was walking by, trying my best not to step on a guy lying in the street. Not paying attention, I ran square into this seven-foot-tall Indian, knocking myself solidly to the pavement.

The man picked me up, shouting, "You're picking on me!"

I thought to myself, "I wouldn't pick on you even if I wanted to. You're too big!" He was obviously quite drunk and in an ugly mood, so I quickly apologized.

"I'm s-s-sorry," I stuttered. "I didn't mean to bump into you; it was an accident."

"It wasn't an accident! You hit me on purpose!" Oh boy, was I in trouble.

"No, I didn't. It was an accident!"

The Indian picked me up by my shirt, lifting me until my feet were dangling. "Please," I squeezed the word out of my constricted vocal chords. "Is it okay if you let me down? I really didn't mean to bump into you."

If looks could kill, I'd be a goner. With his black eyes boring holes through my face, he slowly put me down, keeping a viselike grip on my arm so I couldn't run away.

FRI_{Day} 12

"Come on," he bellowed. "Let's go have a drink together."

"Why don't we just take a walk around the block and get some fresh air," I suggested, praying I wouldn't upset the huge man again.

The man agreed that walking sounded like a pretty good idea, so off he went, dragging me behind him. Not exactly what I had in mind, I thought.

"What's your name?"

"Sun Bear," he replied.

I wasn't sure I'd heard him right, so I asked him again what his name was.

He stopped, turned, looked me right in the eyes, and answered with a condescending pause between each word: "Sun! Bear! And you better not make fun of it!"

"Sun Bear is a nice name," I told him. Frankly, as I looked again at all seven feet, 250 pounds of him, his name could have been Sun Flower and I wouldn't have laughed!

As we walked, Sun Bear began to feel more comfortable with me and told me about his life as an Indian living on the streets. Apparently, there were certain bars that only Indians frequented. "You'd better not go in there. You're a white boy," he warned. I can't say we really had a conversation; it was more like a monologue. Sun Bear talked and I listened.

Finally he paused, looked around, and invited me into the nearest bar for a drink. He ordered his drink and cast a bewildered look my way when I said, "I'll take a water, please."

"You don't have enough money to get a real drink? Here, let me buy you one," Sun Bear offered. He pulled each pocket of his pants inside out, and after discovering he was broke, he said I'd have to stick with water.

Several minutes of silence passed as Sun Bear savored every drop of liquor and I sipped my water. Eventually I broke the silence. "Sun Bear, what are you doing here?"

He slammed his drink down hard on the table and stared at the amber liquid. Then he sadly confessed, "This is why I'm here!"

"There's more to it than that, isn't there Sun Bear? Why is it you're here?"

He pulled his chair close to mine, leaned toward me and said, "Someday I'll tell you," indicating that as far as he was concerned, the conversation was over.

Sun Bear looked away from me, lost in his thoughts. I silently asked God if this was an opportunity to share His love. "He is young, big and strong, and could probably find work anywhere," I prayed. "I wonder why he's here and what I can do for him. More importantly, what can You do for him, Lord?"

Sun Bear gulped the last drop from his glass and commanded, "Okay, let's go!" I was glad he still wanted me to walk with him.

The day was young and we had many hours of daylight to head downtown and panhandle for money. Sun Bear had a unique method for getting complete strangers to cough up their spare change. As someone would approach, he'd simply stand up, towering inches—even feet—above them, look sternly down his nose at them, and hold out his hand. Most eagerly emptied their pockets of change and hurried on their way!

Panhandling was good for Sun Bear that day, so he offered to buy me a hamburger. He ordered another drink with lunch.

"Why don't you wait awhile before you start drinking again?" I asked him. "If we're going to spend time together today, I'd like for you to be sober."

"No problem, I can handle that," he replied. But only a few hours passed before he was craving his next drink. We talked about this, and as we did, he admitted he had a drinking problem.

"Sun Bear, you're too young to be out here on the streets. Please tell me what happened. You obviously have abilities and talents that shouldn't be squelched here on skid row." I was trying as tenderly as possible to let him know I truly cared about his life and what had led him to such despair.

Suddenly, Sun Bear began to cry. "Kurt, I've messed up my life. I have really blown it!" Pulling his arm across his face to wipe the tears, he continued, "I'm from an Indian reservation in eastern Washington. I came to the big city to make something of myself—to better myself." How often I had heard that story. "I couldn't find a job, so I ended up here. And now, alcohol is controlling my life. I have to have it. I need it—and I'd do anything to get money to buy it."

"So are you telling me you're an alcoholic?" I knew he needed to admit this and come face to face with the real issue.

"No, no, I'm not an alcoholic," he insisted. "I'm just having some trouble right now."

I decided not to press the issue, and we talked awhile about his home and family. He told me how much he missed being there.

"Why don't you go back where there are people who love you?" I asked.

"I can't go back. My mom thinks I'm holding down a job here. She hasn't even heard from me in three or four months. I don't want to go back and let her see what a failure I've become," he admitted sadly.

"If your mom loves you, she'll understand and support you. Sun Bear, the definition of success is to keep trying and keep trying and keep trying. You can't give up! Your people back home love you, and I want you to know something else. There is a God in heaven who loves you, and He has a plan for your life. With God's help and your family's support, you can make it! You can go back and start over! Sun Bear, I want to encourage you to do that."

It was obvious by the look on his face that the Lord was working in his heart. As the tears continued to flow, he admitted he wanted to go back home and start over. He finally agreed to call his mother, but he wanted me to talk to her first.

"Why are people always trying to get me to talk on the phone?" I thought to myself. They had no idea how intimidated I was—afraid I would stutter so badly that the person on the other end would just hang up. I tried to explain this, but Sun Bear firmly insisted that I go ahead and dial the number.

"Hello," I heard his mother say.

Now, what I tried to say was, "Hello! My name is Kurt, and Sun Bear is here." Of course, it didn't come out that way. I could only make a stuttering sound as Sun Bear's mother hung up on me.

"What happened?" Sun Bear asked.

"I tried to tell you I can't talk on the phone. The words wouldn't come out, and she hung up."

Sun Bear dug into his pocket for more money, and we placed the call again. I was going to concentrate this time and just say "Sun Bear." Maybe then she'd stay on the line. When she answered and heard her son's name, Sun Bear's mother listened while I stuttered my way through an explanation.

Sun Bear was getting excited and kept saying, "Tell her the rest, tell her the rest!" So I told her he loved her and that he was having a difficult time finding a job. Then I told her that alcohol was a big problem in her son's life, but that he wanted to come home and try again if she would let him.

Suddenly Sun Bear grabbed the phone out of my hand. "Mom, it's me!" he cried. Sun Bear spent the next twenty minutes pouring his heart out. I've never seen a man cry as much as he did during that conversation. His heart was absolutely broken.

When he had said all he had to say, he handed me the phone. His mother thanked me for being with her son and for offering him some direction. She said she had been praying for Sun Bear to come back home.

"Are you a Christian?" I asked.

"Yes," she said. I told her that the most important thing Sun Bear needed was a relationship with Christ. She agreed and said, "Please tell him that life without Jesus is hopeless."

My conversation with Sun Bear's mother ended, and as I hung up the receiver, he gave me a great big hug. "She wants me to come back home! Now we've got to raise enough money for a bus ticket," he said as he grabbed my arm and dragged me behind him.

We spent the rest of that day and night, as well as the next day, panhandling for the money. Late the following day we finally had enough money for Sun Bear's ticket home. There was a bus headed for his reservation that very afternoon, and he had to hurry to catch it. Before he left, Sun Bear agreed to keep an open mind about his relationship with Jesus Christ, and he admitted this might be something he needed to take very seriously. Before he left for the bus station, we prayed together, and I was encouraged by his openness.

About four weeks later, I thought I saw a familiar figure walking down Burnside Street. As I drew closer I realized it was Sun Bear! I felt the anger rise within me, knowing that if he was on skid row, it was because he was drinking again.

"Sun Bear, what are you doing here?" I asked incredulously.

When Sun Bear heard my voice, he took off running in the other direction. My anger pumped adrenaline into my system, and I ran fast enough to catch up with the giant man, grab him by the shirt, and pull him down to the ground. Before I could say anything, I noticed the ugly scars on his face. They ran from the bottom of his chin to the top of his nose. There were also cuts that had not yet healed.

"What happened?" I asked.

Through teeth clenched tight with frustration, he spit out the angry words. "I only had five or six blocks to go before I would be at the bus station. A bunch of guys jumped me and beat me up. They stole all my money! That was it. If God did have a direction for my life, why did He allow this to happen? Why? *Why*?"

I was absolutely speechless. I had no answer to offer him. Standing up, I mindlessly straightened my clothing, trying to regain my composure enough to help him understand that God *did* love him. But with a look of disgust and a slight shake of his head, he just turned and walked away.

Sun Bear's questions were some of the toughest I've ever had to face. I prayed that God would place someone in his life to help him. There was nothing else I could do. I felt completely helpless.

This world is Satan's domain. As long as we live in it, bad things will happen. The struggle with Satan will continue for all of us. I realize I need to encourage others continually to keep striving to be like Christ and never give up. When times get tough, when we question why, we can be assured that He loves us. We can know that salvation is ours. But until we are safely in the arms of our heavenly Father, tough times will come. One day, when we see Him face to face, we'll understand why.

Taking It Inward

It's an age-old question: "If God is loving and in control, then why do so many bad things happen?" For many people, this question is the measuring stick by which they gauge Christianity and deem it unworthy of their faith. Sun Bear may have fallen into this category—and it's true, the circumstances of his life seem incredibly unfair.

When Jesus ministered on the earth, He walked closely with twelve men. Within that group of twelve, Jesus was even closer to three disciples—Peter and two brothers, James and John. When Jesus left to be with the Father, these three men became leaders of the young but growing church.

But in Acts 12, the Bible records a sad event in the lives of Peter and James. As you read the passage below, circle every mention of James. Underline every mention of Peter.

Acts 12:1–11

[1] It was about this time that King Herod arrested some who belonged to the church, intending to persecute them. [2] He had James, the brother of John, put to death with the sword. [3] When he saw that this pleased the Jews, he proceeded to seize Peter also. This happened during the Feast of Unleavened Bread. [4] After arresting him, he put him in prison, handing him over to be guarded by four squads of four soldiers each. Herod intended to bring him out for public trial after the Passover.

[5] So Peter was kept in prison, but the church was earnestly praying to God for him. [6] The night before Herod was to bring him to trial, Peter was sleeping between two soldiers, bound with two chains, and sentries stood guard at the entrance. [7] Suddenly an angel of the Lord appeared and a light shone in the cell. He struck Peter on the side and woke him up. "Quick, get up!" he said, and the chains fell off Peter's wrists. [8] Then the angel said to him, "Put on your clothes and sandals." And Peter did so. "Wrap your cloak around you and follow me," the angel told him. [9] Peter followed him out of the prison, but he had no idea that what the angel was doing was really happening; he thought he was seeing a vision.

> [10] They passed the first and second guards and came to the iron gate leading to the city. It opened for them by itself, and they went through it. When they had walked the length of one street, suddenly the angel left him. [11] Then Peter came to himself and said, "Now I know without a doubt that the Lord sent his angel and rescued me from Herod's clutches and from everything the Jewish people were anticipating."

What happened to James? (Write it here.)

What happened to Peter?

Doesn't this seem incredibly unfair? Peter was miraculously rescued, but James was killed. These two men were doing God's work—they had even been best friends with Jesus!

Where did the idea get started that life would be easy as long as God was in control? It obviously didn't come from God. In fact, let's see what else God said about life in this world. You've already read this passage on a previous day, but you need to see how it applies to Sun Bear's question after he was robbed: "If God did have a direction for my life, why did He allow this to happen?"

2 Corinthians 1:3–4

> [3] Praise be to the God and Father of our Lord Jesus Christ, the Father of compassion and the God of all comfort, [4] who comforts us in all our troubles, so that we can comfort those in any trouble with the comfort we ourselves have received from God.

Where does our comfort come from?

FRI_{Day} 12

According to this passage, why do we receive this comfort?

How is God described in verse 3? Write the descriptions word-for-word below.

Based on 2 Corinthians 1:3–4, what is God saying to you about life being easy? (Do you remember John 16:33 from yesterday? Flip back to it and think about this verse before you answer.)

Seal the Deal

Go back to Sun Bear's question, "If God did have a direction for my life, why did He allow this to happen?" How would you use the verses you've just read to minister to someone like Sun Bear? If no one has asked you this question yet, they will! Jot your thoughts in this space.

You may be asking "why?" about something yourself—or maybe close friends are asking this question. God did have a direction for Sun Bear's life, and He promised to comfort and help him overcome any trouble. Thanks to Adam and Eve, we live in a fallen world. So if you want to blame someone for trouble, don't blame God. Blame them—and look to God for help!

Do Day

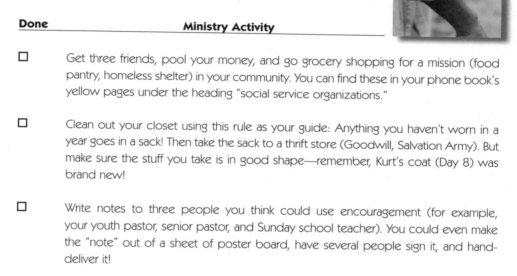

And let us consider how we may **spur one another on** toward **love** and **good deeds**.

—Hebrews 10:24 (emphasis added)

Done   **Ministry Activity**

☐   Get three friends, pool your money, and go grocery shopping for a mission (food pantry, homeless shelter) in your community. You can find these in your phone book's yellow pages under the heading "social service organizations."

☐   Clean out your closet using this rule as your guide: Anything you haven't worn in a year goes in a sack! Then take the sack to a thrift store (Goodwill, Salvation Army). But make sure the stuff you take is in good shape—remember, Kurt's coat (Day 8) was brand new!

☐   Write notes to three people you think could use encouragement (for example, your youth pastor, senior pastor, and Sunday school teacher). You could even make the "note" out of a sheet of poster board, have several people sign it, and hand-deliver it!

Worship

Speak to one another with psalms, hymns and spiritual songs. Sing and make music in your heart to the Lord, always giving thanks to God the Father for everything, in the name of our Lord Jesus Christ.

—Ephesians 5:19–20 (emphasis added)

Take this book to church, and use these pages for taking notes on your worship and learning experiences.

Sunday School
Subject:

Bible passages referred to:

What are at least two things you can begin applying **today** from this lesson?

Worship
Write a prayer (perhaps during the offering time or just before the service begins) that expresses your gratitude for His mercy and grace.

SUN_{Day} 14

Sermon

Subject/Title:

Scripture text:

Key points:

Cool thoughts or observations:

What did God say to you through this sermon?

What is He asking you to change?

Connections

How did God weave together your experiences of the week with your worship and learning today? Take a moment to write down any connections in the space below.

Week 3

Day 15   The Harmonica
Day 16   The Homosexual
Day 17   The Dead Man
Day 18   Cindy's
Day 19   Success
Day 20   Do Day
Day 21   Worship

The Harmonica

It was early in the morning when I woke up. The night before I had made my bed in a garbage bin, so waking up before the garbage truck arrived was important! Many bums have been killed because they were thrown into the garbage truck when the garbage bin was emptied.

I had slept fairly well that night. As I stretched and looked around, I realized that another man had crawled in during the night and was still sound asleep.

"Hey, you'd better get out of here before the garbage truck comes," I said as I shook the man awake.

We climbed out of the garbage bin and walked together down the quiet street. He introduced himself as Mr. Lewis, and I said my name was Kurt. We had walked a little further when he turned to me and said, "I need a drink. Got any money?"

"No," I assured him. "I don't."

"I've got enough for a small bottle of something," he told me. "Why don't you come along?"

I wasn't interested in sharing his liquor, but I was interested in the man. We soon found it was too early for the liquor stores to open, so I talked him into a cup of coffee instead. As we walked, Mr. Lewis pulled a harmonica from his pocket and began to play. It was truly beautiful! "You're really good at that," I told him.

"It takes a lot of practice," he replied. "You want to play it?"

MON_{Day} 15

As he handed me his harmonica, I noticed the tobacco juice all over it and the smell of stale alcohol. "Uh, no thanks," I said as I handed it back.

"Ah, go ahead. Try it!" He pushed the harmonica in my direction again.

I didn't want to offend him, so I put the harmonica to my mouth and attempted to play it. Tasting the tobacco and alcohol that were as much a part of the harmonica as the music it produced, I began to cough and spit. Mr. Lewis just laughed.

"You're not supposed to suck in that hard. The idea is to blow out with smooth, calm breaths." He took the harmonica back and began playing it for me. We laughed together as he finished his melody, dropped it into his pocket, patted it and said, "This is one of my best friends."

"What is?" I asked.

"The harmonica. It soothes me in the evenings when I'm alone and gives me some encouragement to go on. It's always dependable."

I reached into my jacket, patted my chest and said, "I have something here like that, too." He eagerly asked to see it. "Oh, I can't show you," I told him.

"Come on. What are you talking about?" His curiosity was obvious.

I said, "It's not really in my pocket; it's in my heart. It's Jesus Christ. He's dependable. He helps me make it through the night and encourages me through-out the day."

Mr. Lewis threw back his head and laughed heartily. "I thought you really had something in there!" he said. "But Jesus? I've had enough of that stuff to last me a lifetime. You know, I used to do all that churchy stuff."

He went on to tell me about his childhood and about his church experiences growing up. "I tried to be a Christian and follow the Lord. But as I grew up, I left it all behind." Mr. Lewis was silent for a moment. Then he continued, "I started drinking, and before long all I cared about was making money. I wanted to be a millionaire. That was my greatest goal." His voice trailed off a bit. Shaking off whatever memory had come to mind, he said, "Wanting money is what got me on skid row. You see, Kurt, I worked so hard for money that I lost my family. I got caught stealing and lost my job. Things got bad— real bad!"

Mr. Lewis thought the liquor stores were probably open by now, so I walked with him as he searched one out. "You know," he started, "I haven't thought about my childhood in so long. It's kind of nice to reflect back to when times were simple."

"It is fun to reflect on our lives and where we've come from," I agreed, "but it's also sobering to see where we're going."

"Kid," he said, "we aren't going anywhere. We're here to stay!"

I shook my head. "No, I don't believe I'm here to stay. This is a nice place to visit, but there's more to life than living here."

"Some of us don't have a choice," he replied sadly. "You're young enough, Kurt. You can still make something of yourself. I'm too old."

"Mr. Lewis, that's not true! You have a lot of life yet to live. But it's your choice to either waste it away by drinking that stuff you just bought and living here—or making something of what's left of your life."

"It's too tough. I can't do it," he replied.

"I agree with you there. *You* can't do it." He seemed troubled by what I had just told him and shot me an angry look.

"I mean you can't do it alone," I said. "You need some help, and that's why I'm here—to encourage you. I want to offer you hope and ideas for leaving this place. Maybe I can help you find a job and some shelter. Maybe I can get you some help so you never have to let alcohol rule your life again," I said, pointing to the bottle in his hand.

Mr. Lewis pulled the bottle close to him, as if protecting a precious treasure that was about to be taken from him. "No, this is my second best friend," he replied. "My first best friend has never left me, and my second best friend helps me when I need it."

Rain began to fall, and the temperature was dropping fast. We jumped into a doorway for shelter but were soon chased off by the storeowner. We spent much of the day running from doorway to doorway, dodging the raindrops and trying our best to stay warm.

Mr. Lewis drank his liquor so fast, I wondered how he stayed on his feet. By nightfall, he was extremely intoxicated. Thankfully, we found a large canopy over a sidewalk and had arrived early enough that there was still room to sit. Soon we were one huddled mass of humanity, as other bums ran under the canopy for protection from the rain. Many of the men had been drinking all day and were soon asleep.

Quietly, Mr. Lewis began to play his harmonica. The tune he played was "Amazing Grace," and before long, those who were still awake began to hum along with the old familiar hymn. When he finished I said, "You know, Jesus has that amazing grace for you. He gives us new life when we accept Him into our hearts."

"I remember all that," he said sadly. "Those are fond memories."

The man continued to play many songs from his childhood days; then he rested awhile. "Those songs were sung at my church when I was a kid," he said. "Kurt, you know why I left the church? It just didn't do anything for me. I wanted so much more. I wanted a nice house and a nice car. When I got some of that, I wanted more. I wanted a bigger house, a bigger car, and more money. Many Sundays as I sat in church, I wished I were at work making more money. I soon found myself spending seven days a week at work, making more money for more things." After a moment he continued, "But the things never did anything for me either."

"It sounds like you never allowed Jesus to be Lord of your life. Money was your top priority even when you were going to church," I explained. He nodded his head, acknowledging that I was right. "Mr. Lewis, when you make Jesus the Lord of your life, He becomes the focus of all your time and the sole desire of your heart. You learn about Him and try to do what pleases Him. You develop a love relationship with Him."

"Well, all I know is, those are good memories." Mr. Lewis soon fell asleep with a heart full of longing for days squandered and long past.

I was able to spend the next few days with Mr. Lewis. At every street corner there were men who would ask him to play some old song or hymn from the past. Mr. Lewis loved the attention and really hammed it up at times.

At the end of one particularly long day, Mr. Lewis was more intoxicated than usual and became rowdy. One of the bums asked him to repeat a song he had just finished playing. For some reason this angered him and they began to fight, really hurting each other with their blows. Mr. Lewis was getting the worst of it, and I was in between the two men, trying to break it up. Finally I was able to drag him away and find a quiet, secluded place where we could safely fall asleep.

Sometime in the night, Mr. Lewis woke up and attempted to play his harmonica. His face was so badly bruised and cut, I knew playing even the easiest tune had to be painful. Nevertheless, he began to play "Amazing Grace."

"I remember the story of amazing grace, Kurt," he said. "No matter how much we fail God, He's always there, ready to pick us up." He looked at me hopefully and asked, "Do you think He is ready to pick me up again?" Before I could answer he continued, "You know it's really mind boggling to think how this great world started with a big bang!"

I thought to myself what a strange turn the conversation had just taken. "Well," I said, "that's an interesting concept."

"Oh, yes, I forgot. You believe in a God who created it all," he said in a condescending tone.

"Yes, I do," I said, looking up at the sky. "The Bible tells us that God's love is greater than all the stars in the heavens."

For a long time, he just sat there gazing at the night sky. Finally, he turned to me and asked, "Kurt, how can you believe in God?"

"You can only believe in God through faith," I answered. "Faith is believing without seeing and acting on that belief—not only believing there is a God, but also believing He's the Master of the universe. He holds all things together that He creates. He is continually making new life that we can touch and see in the form of flowers and beautiful green grass. He created the very air we breathe. It takes faith to believe that He is the Lord of our lives. He gives us a free will so that we can choose to either believe Him or not. But when we choose to believe, He makes His presence within us undeniable."

I let all of that sink in for a moment, then continued, "Do you remember the butterfly we saw yesterday?" He nodded his head. "That was a beautiful creation of God. It was like a painting in motion—a beautiful, living picture."

He sat there staring at me. He seemed to be soaking up my words like a dry sponge soaks up water.

"Mr. Lewis, if you want to know if God is there, just ask Him to come into your heart. He'll make beautiful things happen there. If you ask, He will take away the guilt and sin and create a beautiful new life within. He did this for me, and He'll do it for you, too."

Mr. Lewis moved his jaw as if he was chewing on something. Thoughtfully he said, "I've been fighting this idea of God for a long time. I had pretty well convinced myself there was no God, but I keep thinking there has to be someone or something in this universe greater than us. There just has to be."

"That's the Holy Spirit prodding you to believe in the Master of the universe, our Savior, Jesus Christ," I explained.

Once again he fixed his gaze on the massive night sky. "There has to be a God to make this such a beautiful place," he said, "but I'm not sure He can make a beautiful thing inside of me. There are a lot of things I've done and terrible things I've gone through. It's too late for me."

I leaned in close to him. "Mr. Lewis, you know what happens to make a butterfly?"

"Of course," he replied. "Everybody knows that."

"No, not everyone," I said. "Tell me."

"Okay," he said and began to impatiently recite the obvious. "There's a caterpillar who makes a little cocoon in a tree and surrounds himself with this cocoon for awhile. Then he turns into a butterfly." His hands spread out, unfolding like wings, and his voice was hushed. Then, almost reverently, he said, "It's a beautiful act of nature, isn't it, Kurt?"

"Oh, yes," I agreed. "We're like a caterpillar that's surrounded by God's love, and in time, through the process of grace, He works with us. God makes us into a beautiful butterfly—a new creation. He alone can give us peace that no man can explain. He alone gives us joy that doesn't need alcohol or material possessions to prime it into being. He alone gives hope for life. Yes, there is Someone bigger than us."

Mr. Lewis was sober now and seemed intent on grasping the meaning of my words. "We're sort of like that caterpillar, struggling along." He shook his head and chuckled softly, "It sure would be nice to be free and fly like a butterfly."

I touched his arm and said, "All you have to do is accept Jesus into your life, ask Him to forgive your sins, and allow Him to be Lord in everything you do—your thoughts, your actions, your desires, and most important to you right now, your future."

"But I don't have a future," he said again. "I've lived here on the streets for more than ten years. I can't even remember what it's like to have a job or a home."

For another fifteen minutes, Mr. Lewis continued to talk about the hopelessness of his life. Finally he grew quiet.

"Jesus wants to be Lord of your future," I told him. "If it's to be here in the streets, He still wants to be Lord of your future. He can make something beautiful out of your life, Mr. Lewis. And you know what? I think you're beautiful already."

For a second, he moved away from me, obviously concerned about my motivation for telling him this.

Laughing, I answered the question on his mind. "No, I'm not," I said. "I just think God sees in you a man who has done some things that are wrong. He sees a man who's hurting inside, a man who wants to be turned into a butterfly—to be set free!"

Mr. Lewis stood up and said, "Let's ponder that thought for awhile. Let's go find something to drink."

I walked with him to a liquor store. He quickly emptied the bottle and went into a drunken rage. I even had to hold him back to keep him from fighting the other bums. It seemed to me he was tortured inside.

Over the next few days, we talked more about God and about survival on the streets. One night, instead of heading for the nearest liquor store, he placed the change he had just panhandled for into his pocket, took my arm, and led me to an alley where other bums were sleeping. It was about 3:00 A.M., and I was exhausted. He told me to stay awake while he slept and then he'd stay awake for me so I could sleep.

While Mr. Lewis slept, I prayed that his heart would be open to receive Jesus' love and salvation. He was more eager to listen than most I had worked with on the streets, and I asked the Lord to speak to him.

The sun was rising before he woke up. He stretched and with a big yawn said, "Let's go get something to drink."

"Hey, what about me! I need a little sleep, too." I could barely keep my eyes open and was desperate for a few hours of sleep.

"I'll get a bottle and come right back to sit here while you sleep," he said.

"Why don't you see if you can make it without a bottle for just one day. Sometimes you're difficult to control when you're drunk," I replied. The exhaustion I was feeling fueled my impatience. I was just too tired to deal with one of his drunken rages and all his endless questions.

Mr. Lewis paced back and forth in anguish. "Oh, Kurt, I appreciate it when you help me, but I need that bottle!" he pleaded.

I looked him straight in the eyes. "Mr. Lewis, you don't need that bottle as much as you think you do. You call it a friend, but in reality, that bottle is your enemy. It gives you a false sense of hope and security. It leaves you with a taste for more and an emptiness you know it can't fill. It's taken everything from you!"

Mr. Lewis looked down the street toward the liquor store and then back at me. I could tell he was in turmoil.

"Okay," he said. "If I go this one day without anything to drink, will you stay with me and help me through it?" I could see the fear and uncertainty in his eyes as he waited for my answer.

"Yes, I will," I promised.

For the next two days, I watched Mr. Lewis fight the most violent battle I'd ever seen. He shook and raged and was completely out of control at times. He

MON_{Day} 15

told me his stomach felt as if it had cramped up in knots. We bought him food from a nearby coffee shop, but nothing seemed to help. I could tell by looking at him that the pain was tremendous.

After two exhausting days, I made him take a walk with me. He followed anxiously behind, afraid to let me out of his sight. We walked toward the river in Portland, to an area that seemed miles from the city. I told Mr. Lewis that I hoped this peaceful place might take his mind off the temptation to buy liquor. It was a long trip on foot; we stopped every half hour or so to let him rest, but finally we reached our destination.

We spent a week beside the river. And it was there that Mr. Lewis made Jesus Christ the Lord of his life. He asked me if I would help him. I told him I would, but that my place was on Burnside Street working with the bums. I suggested that he move, find a job somewhere outside the area, and get some help. There were missions that offered this kind of help to those who were truly sincere about changing their lives. We prayed together and talked for the next few days. We visited a few missions and found one that would take him in and help in the ways he needed. There was great sadness when we finally parted ways. I headed back to Burnside, and Mr. Lewis left it all behind to start a new life. We held hands, prayed, and said good-bye.

As I walked away he said, "Oh, Kurt, wait."

He took out his old harmonica and played a few chords. "I want you to have this," he said as he handed me his most prized possession. "Every time you play it or look at it, I want you to remember me. Remember that I replaced this 'best friend' with my real Best Friend, Jesus. He's really changed my life like you said. Please take it and remember me. Let's keep in touch."

I began to cry as Mr. Lewis placed in my hand an important piece of his life. I knew that harmonica was one of the most valuable things he had on earth; it had given him an escape and some much-needed peace during his days on the cruel streets of skid row. But now he'd replaced it with Jesus—his "number one Friend"…his Friend for eternity.

Taking It Inward

Deception is the Devil's best tool—and he uses it well. Through deception, Satan tries to convince us that everything we need for a good life is here in the world. He makes sinful things **appear** fulfilling and convinces us that we've just gotta have them (or **do** them) in order to be happy. Meanwhile, Jesus patiently says to us, "I've come to give you abundant life." It all boils down to this question: **Who are you going to believe?**

Mr. Lewis was trapped in the web of deception Satan had wound around him. His two "friends," his love of material things, even his thoughts about creation were based on something false. This deception kept Mr. Lewis from believing in the one thing that could give him true life—the gospel of Jesus Christ. The apostle John wrote his gospel for one reason: so that those who read it would believe in Jesus as the Christ and by believing have eternal life.

When the word **believe** was used in the Greek language, it meant to trust something so much that it changed your behavior (your lifestyle, attitudes, and so on). As you read the following verses from John's gospel, keep this definition in mind. Every time you see a form of the word "believe," draw a light bulb [💡] over it. Mark any benefits of believing with a smiley face [☺] and any consequences of not believing with a frowning face [☹].

John 3:10–18

> 10 "You are Israel's teacher," said Jesus, "and do you not understand these things? 11 I tell you the truth, we speak of what we know, and we testify to what we have seen, but still you people do not accept our testimony. 12 I have spoken to you of earthly things and you do not believe; how then will you believe if I speak of heavenly things? 13 No one has ever gone into heaven except the one who came from heaven—the Son of Man. 14 Just as Moses lifted up the snake in the desert, so the Son of Man must be lifted up, 15 that everyone who believes in him may have eternal life.

MON_{Day} 15

> ¹⁶ "For God so loved the world that he gave his one and only Son, that whoever believes in him shall not perish but have eternal life. ¹⁷ For God did not send his Son into the world to condemn the world, but to save the world through him. ¹⁸ Whoever believes in him is not condemned, but whoever does not believe stands condemned already because he has not believed in the name of God's one and only Son.

John 8:23–24

> ²³ But he continued, "You are from below; I am from above. You are of this world; I am not of this world. ²⁴ I told you that you would die in your sins; if you do not believe that I am the one I claim to be, you will indeed die in your sins."

Take a minute to look back at all the smiley faces you marked, and list below every benefit of believing. Then check out your frowning faces, and list the consequences of not believing.

Benefits of Believing   **Consequences of Not Believing**

There it is…black and white…two contrasting columns…benefits and consequences. Circle the column **you** want to experience! Now here's the question: Does your behavior match your belief in Jesus, or are you trapped in some form of deception?

    ☐ Yes! It matches.   ☐ No! I'm trapped.

Are you ready to experience true life, just as Jesus said you could—and see beyond the façade the Enemy has placed in front of you?

John records in his gospel several people who walked in deception until they encountered Jesus. Then they believed, and their lives showed their belief! Through Kurt, the love of God reached Mr. Lewis. When he believed in Jesus as the Christ and Lord of his life, he was able to break away from a destructive lifestyle. He even handed over to Kurt his "best friend" from his old life, his harmonica.

Check out some moments in the Bible when others turned in their "harmonicas" in order to experience the true Friend who sacrificed His life for them. Don't just read the verses referenced here—read what comes before and after to see what led up to the moment of belief. **Who was involved? How did this belief come about? What was said?**

John 2:22   **John 4:39**   **John 9:35–38**   **John 11:25–27**

Seal the Deal

It was a powerful moment when Mr. Lewis handed Kurt his harmonica. If you've decided to believe in Jesus and walk away from a destructive behavior, come up with a plan to "hand" someone your "harmonica."

• Call a trusted friend and ask him or her to keep you accountable to your commitment.

• Select an item that represents the deception you've held on to, and give it to a friend or destroy it.

Maybe you're the trusted friend in someone else's life—someone you know who's trapped in deceptive, destructive behavior. Write the name of that person (or people) below, and pray for them every day for a week.

The Homosexual

Looking back, I know I had asked for this.

I had just finished reading some scriptures written by John, the "apostle of love." I remember praying, "God, if there's anything in my life—or anyone in my life—keeping me from being the best Christian I can be, show me who or what it is. I want to be pleasing in Your sight, so that I can be the best lover of humanity I can be."

The Lord answered my prayer, as He sometimes does, in a way that required extreme action to back up my words.

A week or so had passed since I'd offered that prayer. I was on the street when a man approached me from behind, grabbed my shoulders, and said, "Hey, let's talk."

I turned to see a man much larger than I, obviously a homosexual. As a young boy, I had experienced an attempted rape by a homosexual, so to say that my heart was not full of love for this man would be an understatement. I hated him because of his lifestyle, and my anger toward him was intense.

"I don't want to talk to you!" I exclaimed. "You're weird, and I don't like you!" I remember thinking, "God, this guy is garbage. Run him over with a car; strike him down with lightning."

But as I turned my back to leave, he grabbed me again. "I said I want to talk to you."

Anger and hatred must have been written all over my face. I thought, "God, this guy is the lowest of the low. He's not worthy of life!"

That's when I sensed Jesus saying to me, "I died for him, and I love him as much as I love you."

"No way, Lord!" I argued in my mind. "You can't love him as much as me. He's a weirdo." I was growing more angry as a spiritual battle began to rage within me.

"Kurt," I felt Jesus say, "I want you to love him as I love him."

At that moment I looked at the man, wanting to say, "I hate you! Get away from me." But when I opened my mouth to speak, all that came out was, "I love you."

"Oh, great," I thought. "Now I'm in trouble. I just told this homosexual I loved him!"

"Good," he said. "Let's talk."

I bowed my head, closed my eyes, and prayed, "God, we have a problem here. I don't like this guy, and I definitely don't love him." In the meantime, the man began to shake me, thinking I had fallen asleep! "I know You love him," I continued, "but I don't. I need You to do something *now*!"

With my head still bowed I stood up, still waiting for the answer that would get me out of this mess, when I remembered that less than a week before, I had asked God to show me anything in my life that was keeping me from loving others as I should. Standing here before me, in the form of a gay man, was the answer to my prayer.

"God, I didn't mean *this*!" my insides practically shouted.

Opening my eyes, I began stuttering so fast that I'm sure the man had trouble understanding me. "You want to talk?" I stuttered. "What do you want to talk about?"

"Come to my room and we'll talk," he answered.

"Well, this is just great," I thought. Portland's homosexual community had a reputation for extreme violence. The men would invite other men to their rooms and rape and kill them. I knew if I went to his room, there was a good possibility I'd never come out alive. At the very least, I would be raped.

"I'm not going to your room. If you want to talk, we can talk here," I said.

"No, I want to talk in my room."

We stood there arguing about where we would talk until I closed my eyes again to pray. "God, he wants me to go to his room," I prayed.

"Hey, why do you keep doing that?" the man yelled. "What's going on?"

I continued praying. "I don't know what to do, Lord. I know You love him. Bring someone out to love him."

"I did," God assured me. "I brought you."

"Bring someone else!" I pleaded.

"I chose you." I had my answer.

"God, I want to be the best I can be. I want to be all I can be for Your sake, but this is so hard!"

God spoke to my heart. "Let Me love him through you."

"Okay. I've trusted You all of my life for all kinds of things, and I will trust You on this."

"Come to my room," the man said again.

I followed. I was confident that as we walked, he would get saved and I wouldn't have to go all the way to his room. So with that in mind, I began asking a million questions like rapid fire.

"What's your name?" No answer.

"Are you from the streets?" No answer.

"Have you ever heard about Jesus?" Again, no answer.

When we got to the building he said, "Come on up."

"W-W-W-Wait a minute," I said. "I need to pray."

"Why do you keep doing that?" He was beginning to get very impatient with me.

"God, now is a good time for Your second coming—or an ice storm or anything You want to do! But Lord, I trust You. Teach me to love him like You love him. I can only do that through Your power." As I opened my eyes, I was filled with the peace that comes only from God. I looked at the big man and said, "I'm ready."

As I walked through the door, I took one look back at skid row—at the men lying on the sidewalks, at the trash in the gutters. I realized how much I would miss all of this if I never came back. Walking up the steps, I prayed, "God, if You loved him enough to die for him, I'll love him, too."

At the top of the steps the man rang a buzzer. An old woman came out of one of the rooms, swearing as she walked. He gave her a five dollar bill in exchange for a key. We continued until we came to his door. He unlocked the door and said, "Come on in."

Immediately I began looking for a way of escape. There was just one window, and it was covered by bars to keep the drunks from falling out. Placing my hand against the window, I mumbled, "Oh, great. God, do a miracle *now*!"

I heard the door lock behind me, and I turned to see the man walk over to the bed, pull back the blankets, and sit down. He patted the bed beside him and said, "Come to bed and let's talk."

I closed my eyes one more time and said, "God, I know it wasn't easy for You to send your Son to the cross. I know it wasn't easy for You to love me. Help me love this man."

The man continued to pat the bed in anticipation, and I knew it was now or never. "Let me tell you about Jesus Christ," I said, realizing my voice had changed. Now there was no contempt, only compassion.

I told the man every Bible verse I knew. I began to explain the scriptures to him, recounting everything from Noah to Revelation, but nothing seemed to be getting through. He just sat there, patting the bed beside him. Nothing was working.

I talked for over an hour. My throat was parched and I was getting tired, but I knew God was going to work a miracle. Anger began to creep into my voice again. "Okay," I demanded, "I've given you the most important information you'll ever get in your life! Now, what are you going to do about it?"

Slowly the man reached inside his shirt and brought out a knife. I was sure my life was about to end. But instead of attacking me, he thrust the knife into the bedpost.

"I was going to rape and kill you tonight," he said. "Some guy was passing out Bible tracts the other night, and I beat him to a pulp. Here you are talking about the same God. Maybe He's trying to tell me something."

"Yes, He is! He is!" I screamed. "He's trying to tell you He loves you. Not only that, I love you!" He just sat and stared at me. "Yes, I do," I continued. "I love you *because* God loves you. I came here with you because I love you. Love is why Christ died on the cross for you."

The man dropped his head and his face grew red. Tears welled up in his eyes as he said, "God can't love me. You have no idea what I've done."

"I can imagine," I told him. "But God can change your life. He's changed mine."

"Do you really believe that?"

"That's why I'm here," I answered. "And believe me, that is the *only* reason I'm here. Love compels me to tell you about Jesus."

The man stood and walked over to where I was. Putting out his hand, he said, "I want to thank you for coming here to talk to me." He took my hand, led me to the door and said, "Get out of here!" I wasted no time.

As the door began to close behind me, I turned and stopped it with my foot. "I want to tell you one more time. God loves you. He's not giving up on you."

As I walked down the steps I heard that huge man fall on the bed, sobbing. I ran out as fast as I could, thankful to be alive. Once outside I prayed, "God, I love that man. I know You do, too. Thank You for helping me love others as You do."

Taking It Inward

Scripture tells us that loving those who love us back is easy. But loving those we're tempted to hate is the kind of love God requires from those who follow Him. To teach Kurt the power of unconditional love, God used someone who represented the bottom of the barrel as far as the unlovable go. This man was an "enemy" who intended to kill Kurt. His presence alone reminded Kurt of a horrible incident from the past.

Let God speak to your heart about loving the unlovable people around you. Printed here are some words from Jesus on the subject. In Matthew 25, the disciples were curious about the end times and asked their local authority on the subject, Jesus. Jesus used some parables to explain what the end will be like—and then He told them **exactly** how it will be. The part you're reading here isn't a parable. It's the real deal!

Find a quiet place and let Jesus' instructions sink deep into your heart. To help you interact with Jesus' words, circle the actions of the King (the Son of Man) as you read. Then underline all the helpless conditions the King experienced.

Matthew 25:31–46

31 "When the Son of Man comes in his glory, and all the angels with him, he will sit on his throne in heavenly glory. 32 All the nations will be gathered before him, and he will separate the people one from another as a shepherd separates the sheep from the goats. 33 He will put the sheep on his right and the goats on his left. 34 "Then the King will say to those on his right, 'Come, you who are blessed by my Father; take your inheritance, the kingdom prepared for you since the creation of the world. 35 For I was hungry and you gave me something to eat, I was thirsty and you gave me something to drink, I was a stranger and you invited me in, 36 I needed clothes and you clothed me, I was sick and you looked after me, I was in prison and you came to visit me.'

> 37 "Then the righteous will answer him, 'Lord, when did we see you hungry and feed you, or thirsty and give you something to drink? 38 When did we see you a stranger and invite you in, or needing clothes and clothe you? 39 When did we see you sick or in prison and go to visit you?' 40 "The King will reply, 'I tell you the truth, whatever you did for one of the least of these brothers of mine, you did for me.' 41 "Then he will say to those on his left, 'Depart from me, you who are cursed, into the eternal fire prepared for the devil and his angels.
>
> 42 For I was hungry and you gave me nothing to eat, I was thirsty and you gave me nothing to drink, 43 I was a stranger and you did not invite me in, I needed clothes and you did not clothe me, I was sick and in prison and you did not look after me.' 44 "They also will answer, 'Lord, when did we see you hungry or thirsty or a stranger or needing clothes or sick or in prison, and did not help you?' 45 "He will reply, 'I tell you the truth, whatever you did not do for one of the least of these, you did not do for me.' 46 "Then they will go away to eternal punishment, but the righteous to eternal life."

In the Sermon on the Mount, Jesus gave some specific instructions about loving a particular group of people. Read the next passage, circling the people you're to love and underlining anything else Jesus said to do for these people.

Matthew 5:43–48

> 43 "You have heard that it was said, 'Love your neighbor and hate your enemy.' 44 But I tell you: Love your enemies and pray for those who persecute you, 45 that you may be sons of your Father in heaven. He causes his sun to rise on the evil and the good, and sends rain on the righteous and the unrighteous. 46 If you love those who love you, what reward will you get? Are not even the tax collectors doing that? 47 And if you greet only your brothers, what are you doing more than others? Do not even pagans do that? 48 Be perfect, therefore, as your heavenly Father is perfect."

Did you make a connection between verse 44 and the first part of verse 45? Looking at these verses from Matthew, what is God stressing about having a relationship with Him?

Now let's put it all together. In these two passages, we see quite a list of people we're supposed to love. Use the chart below to record each type of person Jesus mentioned. Then record the action we're to do toward those people. We've supplied you with an example from each passage.

Types of People	Actions toward the People
hungry (25:35)	feed them (25:35)
enemies (5:44)	love them (5:44)

Ministering to others is a big thing with God! What do you think He's looking for from us? (Check all that apply.)

- ☐ to have a lifestyle of ministry to others
- ☐ to do an occasional service project
- ☐ just to pray for people in need and those who serve
- ☐ to send some money for those in need
- ☐ to feel concern for the helpless

Seal the Deal

Is what we're talking about simply "a good thing to do"—or is it a requirement for those who want to be in God's kingdom? Be honest. Over the past six months, have you been more of a "sheep" or a "goat"? (See Matthew 25:32–36.)

Listed on the next page are the helpless situations mentioned in Matthew and some modern-day parallels of each. Beneath each situation, write some ministries or individuals you could reach out to. These could be in your family, community, or church.

TUE_{Day} 16

- The hungry or thirsty—The homeless, the impoverished, those lacking basic necessities.

- The strangers—The lonely, those in nursing homes, widows/widowers.

- Those in need of clothes—The impoverished, the homeless, single-parent families.

- The sick—Those in hospitals, the terminally ill.

- Those in prison—Those in juvenile detention centers or jails, those trapped in depression or spiritual bondage.

How can you make God's instructions to minister to these people more than an occasional project, but instead, a lifestyle? Listen for God's voice as you follow Him this week.

The Dead Man

Ambulances and police cars were a common sight on skid row. They'd often arrive to pick up those who had died during the night from a drug or alcohol overdose, or from falling through the floor of an old building. Sometimes these forgotten men and women lay in old buildings for several days without being missed or noticed, until another drunk, searching for shelter, would stumble upon the body.

It seemed to me that death was as common as life on skid row. In many ways, even men who were physically alive were dead emotionally and spiritually. More than anything, I desired to have the chance to offer the hope of Jesus, and I was always heartbroken to hear of another person dying without that hope.

One night while seeking shelter, I descended the steps leading under the Burnside Bridge. The loud echo of my every step reminded me how alone I was that night. Soon I heard the echo of my own loud gasp as I saw a man lying motionless on the cold concrete below. I moved to help him but quickly realized it was too late. He was already dead.

I had never before seen or touched a dead body. Startled and afraid, I had no idea what to do. I could hear my heart pounding blood through my veins, and I took a deep breath to regain my composure. Soon any fear was replaced with compassion and sorrow for this poor lost soul. Sitting down on the last step, I gently placed his head in my lap.

How sad to die there in the cold with an empty liquor bottle as your only companion! As I waited there, trying to decide what I should do, I thought of how much God loved this man. I wished I could have known him to tell him of

God's remarkable love and how it could have changed him forever. I wondered if it would have made a difference.

"There's so much unnecessary death here," I thought, my chest constricted with sorrow. I sat there with him for a very long time.

Eventually I ran up the steps to search for a policeman. I found one sitting in his car several blocks away. "There's a dead man under the bridge; he's lying at the bottom of the steps," I told him, confident he'd handle the situation right away. The officer thanked me and drove off.

I walked the streets for hours that night, trying to get the image of the dead body out of my mind—yet feeling compelled to never really forget the lonely image of the man who'd died with no hope. Four hours passed as I walked and thought about this unnecessary death.

Later I returned to the bridge for shelter from the increasing cold of the night. As I started down the same steps where I had found the body, I couldn't believe my eyes. Lying there, after four hours, was the same dead man. No one had come to collect the body!

I hurried down the steps to chase away the rats that already surrounded the body, furious with the police—or the system—that seemed not to care about the street people. I remembered the policeman asking if the man was a bum or a drunk, and suddenly I realized he was trying to put a value on this man's life. Was he worth hurrying for—or could it wait? Obviously the dead man didn't care, but I did. It bothered me to think that if this were a well-dressed businessman who had accidentally fallen and died, someone would have been there within five minutes. Because this was a drunken bum, there was no reason to hurry.

I went back up to the street and found another police officer. I told him, "There's a dead man under the bridge. I've reported this once already, and no one has come to pick up the body."

Annoyed, he replied, "We'll get to it when we can."

There was nothing else to do, so I returned to the man and stayed there until the ambulance arrived an hour or so later. I asked the attendants what they would do with the body. They said more than likely he would be cremated.

I stood silently as the ambulance pulled away. That was it. That was the end of this man's life. He had moved unacknowledged through the streets, and he had died with no one to grieve his passing. He would be remembered only for as long as it took for the ashes of his body to be scattered on the wind.

"Lord," I prayed, "help me to value life so that no one near me dies without some sorrow expressed—and without my understanding afresh Your value of that person."

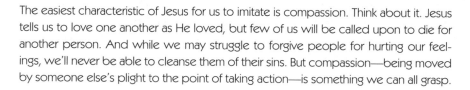

Taking It Inward

He who oppresses the poor shows contempt for their Maker, but whoever is kind to the needy honors God.
—Proverbs 14:31

The easiest characteristic of Jesus for us to imitate is compassion. Think about it. Jesus tells us to love one another as He loved, but few of us will be called upon to die for another person. And while we may struggle to forgive people for hurting our feelings, we'll never be able to cleanse them of their sins. But compassion—being moved by someone else's plight to the point of taking action—is something we can all grasp.

When Kurt realized that the motionless body under the bridge was a man who had died alone, he was overwhelmed with compassion. The scriptures that follow record moments when others had similar experiences of being overwhelmed with compassion. As you read these verses, circle the words "compassion" and "mercy." Then use the exercises that follow to think about how you can imitate this wonderful characteristic of Jesus.

Luke 10:29–37

29 But he wanted to justify himself, so he asked Jesus, "And who is my neighbor?" 30 In reply Jesus said: "A man was going down from Jerusalem to Jericho, when he fell into the hands of robbers. They stripped him of his clothes, beat him and went away, leaving him half dead. 31 A priest happened to be going down the same road, and when he saw the man, he passed by on the other side. 32 So too, a Levite, when he came to the place and saw him, passed by on the other side.

33 But a Samaritan, as he traveled, came where the man was; and when he saw him, he took pity on him. 34 He went to him and bandaged his wounds, pouring on oil and wine. Then he put the man on his own donkey, took him to an inn and took care of him. 35 The next day he took out two silver coins and gave them to the innkeeper. 'Look after him,' he said, 'and when I return, I will reimburse you for any extra expense you may have.' 36 "Which of these three do you think was a neighbor to the man who fell into the hands of robbers?" 37 The expert in the law replied, "The one who had mercy on him." Jesus told him, "Go and do likewise."

Matthew 9:35–38

35 Jesus went through all the towns and villages, teaching in their synagogues, preaching the good news of the kingdom and healing every disease and sickness. 36 When he saw the crowds, he had compassion on them, because they were harassed and helpless, like sheep without a shepherd. 37 Then he said to his disciples, "The harvest is plentiful but the workers are few. 38 Ask the Lord of the harvest, therefore, to send out workers into his harvest field."

Matthew 14:13–14

13 When Jesus heard what had happened, he withdrew by boat privately to a solitary place. Hearing of this, the crowds followed him on foot from the towns. 14 When Jesus landed and saw a large crowd, he had compassion on them and healed their sick.

Mark 6:34

34 When Jesus landed and saw a large crowd, he had compassion on them, because they were like sheep without a shepherd. So he began teaching them many things.

Luke 7:12–15

12 As he approached the town gate, a dead person was being carried out—the only son of his mother, and she was a widow. And a large crowd from the town was with her. 13 When the Lord saw her, his heart went out to her and he said, "Don't cry." 14 Then he went up and touched the coffin, and those carrying it stood still. He said, "Young man, I say to you, get up!" 15 The dead man sat up and began to talk, and Jesus gave him back to his mother.

The next step is key. In fact, take a minute to ask God to open your eyes to the heart of Jesus as you meditate on these passages.

Okay, here we go. Look over the passages you just read, and find the words you circled. Then find the answers to the questions in the chart below. Be sure to write the answers in the space provided.

	Who had compassion?	Who received compassion and what was the need?	What did the compassion-giver do?
Luke 10			
Matthew 9			
Matthew 14			
Mark 6			
Luke 7			

WED Day 17

Of the people who received compassion in these passages, who does your heart break for the most?

Do you know anyone in a similar situation? Who?

Seal the Deal

What can you do to imitate what Jesus did for the people on whom He had compassion? Obviously, you can't raise them from the dead, but you **can** imitate Jesus' heart and attitude when He encountered each person. In the space here, write two or three actions you can take to show mercy or compassion. Then pick an action and do it between now and your next meal!

My Actions

Cindy's

Sexual temptation is big these days, as it was when I was a college student and worked and lived part-time on the streets. Skid row, as with the seedy side of any town, was teeming with massage parlors, which are houses of prostitution. Since the Bible says to avoid the very appearance of evil, I avoided even walking past these places.

What went on inside these evil establishments was bad enough, but when business was slow, the prostitutes would stand out on the street and solicit the men passing by. "Here I am," they'd shout. "I'm available!"

Temptations naturally came along, but I determined never to make myself vulnerable. My testimony did and still does mean everything to me. My entire ministry could have been ruined had I given in to the temptation of illicit sex. I was determined to keep myself pure—for God and for my future wife.

"Cindy's" was the name of a massage parlor where men paid money for female companionship and sexual favors. Early one afternoon I noticed that the girls from Cindy's were standing in front of their house. Obviously, business was slow. As usual, I avoided the whole scene by walking on the other side of the street. But though I tried not to even look in their direction, I found myself doing it anyway. Instead of lust and temptation, I felt incredible compassion for these girls—young women who were willing to be used up for a dollar. How sad to realize these women had so little self-worth. They were merely a commodity to be sold to the highest bidder. "How devastated their souls must be," I thought.

I noticed a young girl sitting away from the other women. She was very attractive, and I found it hard to believe she could be a prostitute. Continuing to walk at a safe distance, I resolved to put the girl out of my mind. But it wasn't working. As I worked with the bums that day, I kept finding the girl in my

thoughts. I decided the best way to handle this was to pray about her. Wrestling with my thoughts, I prayed, "Lord, please remove this from my mind; I don't want anything to do with her. I want to avoid all temptation." When my mind wouldn't let go, I found a quiet place to be alone and talk to God.

"Lord, what is it about this girl that makes me unable to forget her?" I asked. "Forgive me, Lord, if it's anything impure. I pray You will give me wisdom."

Sometimes when we're seeking to know God's will, it helps to consult our Christian friends, and I felt led to do this. There weren't many people on skid row who fell into that category. But back on campus I had a core group of friends who knew about the street ministry and were avid prayer warriors for this cause. I went back to school to find them.

The long walk to campus gave me time to meditate on my struggle and try to make sense of it all. I was certain that if I could just get her out of my mind, everything would be fine. I could return to the streets to work with the bums. But all the way home, the girl's eyes, the expression on her face, and the sense of pity I felt for her seemed to intensify. I kept asking myself, "Why would she sell herself? Why would she be in that place?"

When I returned to campus, I found my friend Fred, in whom I had great confidence. I always valued his insights. Fred listened intently to my every word, and I'm sure he also heard my heart. After a few silent moments he said, "Kurt, after listening to what you just shared—and knowing your desire to please God, stay pure, and resist temptation—I think you should go with what you're feeling. Maybe God *wants* you to go back and talk to this girl."

We talked and prayed some more, and I decided to trust God and see what He had in store. Fred reached into his pocket. "Here's enough money for a bus ticket. If you feel this is what God wants, go back and talk to the girl."

As I left campus on the bus back to skid row, I felt an assurance that the Lord had put this girl on my heart for an important reason. I was to find her and tell her about His love for her. My friends committed to bathe me and my situation in prayer, and I felt strengthened. I knew my motivation for seeing her was pure and that God was in it.

There were no girls on the street when I arrived at Cindy's. That meant I would have to go inside. It was my very first time in a massage parlor, and the darkness—both literal and figurative—almost made me vomit. I was sure this was what Sodom and Gomorrah must have been like. It was a place where nothing but sensual pleasures were being gratified. I became incredibly aware of the spiritual destruction occurring there, and I knew I was seeing it all with God's eyes.

The girls were sitting on couches when I entered, and I immediately spotted the young girl. God's timing is perfect, and I knew that was why she wasn't busy when I got there.

The woman I assumed was in charge asked what I wanted. "I'd like to talk to that girl over there," I replied. She looked at me coldly and told me what it would cost. "No, I just want to talk to her, if I could."

"No one talks to the girls unless they pay," came her reply. It was obvious she meant business.

"But all I want to do is talk. Really."

"You can talk to her after you pay!" she snapped.

The girl could overhear what we were saying. She probably wondered who I was and what I wanted.

"Either you pay or you leave!" the woman demanded.

I only had enough money to get home on the bus—not nearly the amount she demanded. I was uncomfortable just being there, and my spirit was in conflict with the spirit that filled that place, so I left.

"Okay, the Lord closed that door. I'm out of here," I thought to myself. I was greatly relieved—for a time.

I began walking around the neighborhood, saying hello to some of my street friends. But again, the girl kept coming back to mind. I decided I should get back to school and immerse myself in schoolwork. I felt certain that becoming wrapped up in my studies would free my mind of the girl.

Back on campus, I found Fred and told him what had happened. Surprised, he said, "Here." He pressed more money into my hand. "Take this and go back. You need to talk to that girl!"

"I just don't think I can do it, Fred."

"You need to if the Lord is speaking to you," he pleaded. "Don't miss this opportunity."

So I took the money from my friend and went again to see if I could talk with her. All my friends agreed to stay up and pray for me until I contacted them.

It was very late by the time the bus dropped me off near Cindy's. I knew the chances of the girl still being there were slim. Frankly, I was praying she wouldn't be there. I wanted to avoid the entire encounter and get back to life as usual.

But as I entered the building, the only one sitting on the couch was—you guessed it—the girl. She was by far the most attractive, yet she had not been requested by any customers. I knew if another man were to walk in, my chance to talk to her would be gone.

The owner came into the room, and the sight of me provoked her. "You again! Did you bring money this time?"

"Yes," I said. "But I just want to talk to her right here in the open hallway."

To my dismay the woman said, "No, you can't talk to her here. You need to go back into one of the rooms."

I argued with her to no avail. She would not let me talk to the young girl out in the open. I tried another tactic. "What if I talk to her outside, in front of the building?"

"You talk to her in one of the rooms—or not at all!" the woman bellowed.

The girl was introduced to me as Pam, and I followed her to a room. In the room was a large bed, and I sat on the edge of it. She sat down beside me and asked, "What would you like?"

This was an incredibly uncomfortable situation, and I wanted it over with as quickly as possible.

"I'd like for you to answer some questions," I told her. I silently prayed and asked the Holy Spirit to speak through me—to anoint me so that the words would flow easily and be understood. This did not happen. I stuttered terribly; the words seemed to tumble out at random and made no sense whatsoever. I wanted Pam to know that I was concerned about her as a person. I managed to say, "Since I saw you this morning, I haven't been able to get you out of my mind. I know you have the potential to become more than you are right now. There is Someone who has a great plan for your life. His name is Jesus Christ."

She listened very politely to all I was telling her. Suddenly she got up and left me in that horrible room alone. I prayed out loud, "Lord, I don't know what I'm doing here. Please, do something." That's when I realized I felt absolutely no temptation. "Thank You," I whispered. I knew that the Lord was ministering to me, as well as to Pam.

After a little while, the girl returned. The woman in charge was behind her. She peeked in the door, then shut it. Pam sat down and quietly asked, "Is that all you wanted, or is there more?"

"No," I said. "I want to leave you with one thought. The life you are leading will only bring you to a dead end. Not only physically, Pam, but it will destroy you emotionally. More than that, I'm concerned about you spiritually.

Here on earth we make decisions that determine how we live and whom we choose to follow. People who come here are following their own selfish desires, Pam. I want you to know that there are many people like me who love God and can testify to the fact that Jesus gives us life and complete fulfillment. There's no need for this stuff. I don't understand why you're here, and I don't know if my coming here will make any difference, but I—"

"I appreciate what you're saying," she interrupted. "My boyfriend and I are trying to save money to build a new house, and this type of work pays me very well. It's worth it in order for us to have that. If I didn't do this, we wouldn't have enough money to build the house."

Amazed by this, I said, "Your *boyfriend* knows you're here?"

"Yes," she replied. "We live together and he approves of this."

"Don't you think he might be using you?" I couldn't believe what I was hearing.

"He loves me. He doesn't mind me doing this."

I looked at her for a moment and said, "If I loved a woman, I wouldn't want her giving herself to other men."

We continued to talk, and I told her how difficult it was for me to understand her perspective. She said she appreciated my concern, and I left feeling that I had accomplished absolutely nothing.

As I walked out of the room Pam said, "I usually don't work today. Someone was out and I worked her shift. It's strange you came looking for me today and found me."

"See," I pleaded, "that's another sign that the Lord really wanted you to be here so I could talk with you. The main thing I want you to hear, Pam, is that Jesus loves you. He has a plan for your life. Follow His plan, not the desires of this world, and He will lead you to fulfillment and happiness."

She stopped me again and thanked me. "How can I remember you?" she asked.

I had a pocket New Testament that I always carried with me. I gave it to her and wrote my name and phone number inside. I reminded her that I'd be praying for her when the Lord brought her to mind. "I will pray that you find a new life in Christ, one that leads to true happiness," I promised and quickly left. "Mission accomplished," I thought to myself.

I returned to skid row a week later to find Cindy's closed down. The story from my friends on the street was that the police raided the establishment. Several girls went to jail, while others were given the option of leaving town. I don't know what happened to Pam, but I know the Lord used me to plant a seed in her life. Maybe it was because she only had a week left there—or maybe it was because something was about to happen in her life and she needed to be confronted. The Lord gave me the opportunity to talk to her, and I'm thankful I listened. I praise God that He worked out every detail of this encounter. The results were up to Him.

Dear Lord, I pray that You will clearly show us Your will—who to speak with and minister to, even if it's outside the normal arena of our lives. I pray for faith that You will take care of every detail in these opportunities. Help me, Lord. Remind me that You are still working in the lives of others, and that sometimes, though I cannot see the purpose or the results, Your Holy Spirit is still active. Amen.

Taking It Inward

When we minister to others, sometimes we think we want results worse than God does! But every spiritual milestone that happens—either in us or in the people we minister to—is a result of the work of God. Our job is simply to obey what God puts before us and trust the Holy Spirit for the results.

THU_{Day} 18

You could see how God orchestrated events so that Kurt could share the gospel with Pam. But as much as Kurt wanted to reap a harvest, it wasn't his job to get Pam into a relationship with Christ. It **was** his job to introduce Pam to the **idea** of a relationship with Jesus—then **trust God** for the harvest. One thing we know: God wants **everyone** to know Him. We can trust Him to complete the process.

The apostle Paul helped start a church in the city of Corinth. Another great teacher, Apollos, helped the church grow. The church grew fast, but the people were apparently expressing their appreciation to these men rather than to God. In one of his letters to this church, Paul helped steer the people's hearts in the right direction. He also explained the principle Kurt learned with Pam, about how God uses people to plant seeds for His harvest.

As you read the passage below, do this:
- Draw a cloud [☁] around every mention of God. Underline anything God does.
- Circle every mention of Paul. Since he wrote this letter, look for words like "I" and "me."
- Using another color, circle every mention of Apollos.

1 Corinthians 3:1–11

1 Brothers, I could not address you as spiritual but as worldly—mere infants in Christ. 2 I gave you milk, not solid food, for you were not yet ready for it. Indeed, you are still not ready. 3 You are still worldly. For since there is jealousy and quarreling among you, are you not worldly? Are you not acting like mere men? 4 For when one says, "I follow Paul," and another, "I follow Apollos," are you not mere men?

5 What, after all, is Apollos? And what is Paul? Only servants, through whom you came to believe—as the Lord has assigned to each his task. 6 I planted the seed, Apollos watered it, but God made it grow. 7 So neither he who plants nor he who waters is anything, but only God, who makes things grow. 8 The man who plants and the man who waters have one purpose, and each will be rewarded according to his own labor.

9 For we are God's fellow workers; you are God's field, God's building. 10 By the grace God has given me, I laid a foundation as an expert builder, and someone else is building on it. But each one should be careful how he builds. 11 For no one can lay any foundation other than the one already laid, which is Jesus Christ.

Look back at what you marked, and in the chart below, write down everything Paul said about himself. Then write what you learn about Apollos—as well as what you learn about Paul and Apollos together. Finally, write what you discovered about God. This may seem like a lot to keep track of, but you're up to it! And God will reward your diligence.

Paul

Apollos

Both Paul and Apollos

God

What does this tell you about how God uses people to accomplish His work?

How did Paul's and Apollos's roles compare with God's role in helping this church become spiritually mature?

What did it all boil down to in verses 10 and 11?

THU Day 18

Seal the Deal

Are you a "planter" or a "waterer"? Chances are, you're a planter in one situation and a waterer in another. In the space below, record the names of people in whom God may be using you to plant a seed. Then jot the names of people you're helping to grow.

Seeds I'm Helping to Plant   **Seeds I'm Watering**

Read 1 Corinthians 3:8–11 again. Then use these verses to pray for the people you've listed. Beside each name, journal a way you can plant or water a seed in this person's life.

Success

God frequently uses people in unpredictable ways to provide for the needs of the outcast. One of the people God used in this manner is Timothy.

Late one night I spotted a man in the distance pushing a grocery cart. His clothes were new and clean, which automatically made me curious about him. As I got closer and could see the contents of his cart, I recognized the familiar logo of a well-known fast-food restaurant. He had a cart full of hamburgers! "No way," I thought. "Not here on skid row."

As I came closer, the man reached into his cart for two hamburgers and gave them to me. I was taken completely off guard and had to know what he was doing there on the streets, giving hamburgers away.

"I hope you enjoy them," he simply said. Then he turned and started to walk away.

I called to him, "Sir, can I go with you?"

He smiled, "Sure, you can help me hand these out."

"To whom?" I asked.

"To anybody who wants one," he answered.

I observed him closely as we passed out hamburgers to the guys on the street. He seemed to genuinely love these men. After the burgers were all distributed, the man prepared to leave.

"Thanks for helping me," he said. He stopped pushing the cart, looked back at me and asked, "Would you like to talk?"

"Sure," I replied, anxious to find out more about him.

We sat on the porch step of a nearby building. He asked my name, what I was doing there, and how I was getting along on the streets. He was truly surprised when I told him I was not one of the homeless, but was living on the streets with the bums to give them encouragement and love. He said his name was Timothy and told me this story.

"I was a homeless man who was ministered to by a group of people who were living on the streets. Missions supported them. There are several of them on skid row now, and they do good work. I'm the product of a mission. Most derelicts think of missions as a place to get a free meal. The real purpose of a mission is to present the gospel to men who are in need. Most missions are disliked because you have to listen to a sermon before you're fed. If it didn't happen in that order, the bums would eat the meals and leave.

"I went to such a mission, as I had done several times before, and I listened to the sermon so I could have a hot meal. Most of the time it was meaningless to me because I was drunk and unable to concentrate on what was being said. This one evening, however, was different. While I was eating, the pastor came over and sat down next to me.

"He asked about my life. We began to talk, but I really didn't want to be bothered. At first, I felt I should at least answer his questions; then an odd thing happened. I began to feel genuine concern from him. His tone of voice and sincerity made me think he really cared about me.

"All the other people in the mission were leaving, but the pastor and I were still talking. I told him about my past life—how I'd been a successful businessman with a beautiful home, a wife, and kids. I also confessed to him about my need for alcohol—how I used to go home from all the pressures at work and have a few drinks to relax. Then I started needing a drink in the morning to gain enough courage to go to work. At work, I needed a drink to keep me going.

Soon I'd become an alcoholic. I needed it to sustain my life. Alcohol was the main reason I lost my job, and it was also the reason my family left me. Skid row was the only place for me to go and keep up my alcohol addiction. I lived on skid row for six long years.

"The pastor told me, 'It sounds like your life is a mess now. You know, Timothy, Jesus gives new life. It takes a lot of work to overcome alcoholism. But if you want to change your life, you can. Are you prepared, Timothy, for eternity?'

"I had heard that same pitch before, but it never really got through to me like it did then. As we talked, I realized what a disaster my life had become. I had never really thought about the possibility of eternal life before. As I sat there listening, I began to think that maybe there was a chance for me. I was bewildered and didn't really know how to answer the pastor's question. I left without giving him an answer.

"Time passed, but I couldn't stop thinking about that pastor's question. I found myself drawn back to the mission. I had to hear more.

"I found the pastor washing dishes in the back of the mission and asked if he had time to talk to me. I helped him finish the dishes and clean the kitchen, and then we sat down together.

"We talked for a long time, and I asked him many questions. Finally, he said, 'Timothy, when you're ready to think about eternity, let me know.' And he got up from the table and walked away.

"That pastor always seemed to let me think things through. He never pushed anything on me, and I believe that's the reason I found myself returning once again to the mission. I confessed to him that I desperately needed something to make sure my eternity was secured in heaven.

"That beloved man led me to the Lord that night. He found a small room for me at the mission and then spent the first three or four weeks with me, helping me while I fought my battle with alcohol. He was with me night and day, caring for me, holding me, encouraging me, and making sure I was keeping my promise to serve the Lord.

"Those first few weeks were hell, but it's been almost four years now since I turned my life over to the Lord. I'm a living testimony to what God can do for people if they have a sincere desire to change their lives. God doesn't promise success in financial terms, but he promises to be with us throughout our lives, here and in eternity.

"I've blown it a couple of times over the years, but the pastor was patient with me and always showed love toward me. I saved a little bit of money as I worked around the mission and soon got a job as a janitor at a nearby fast-food restaurant. The pastor allowed me to keep the room at the mission for low rent, which helped me save my earnings.

"Before long, I moved up from janitor to cook. Then I moved from the cook's position to handling the money in the front and waiting on customers. Because of my prior experience in management, I was able to help by hiring and training personnel. I ended up being one of the night managers.

"I still lived at the mission and continued to save as much money as I could. About three years later, the restaurant was being sold to a private firm. A couple of the managers asked if I wanted to go into partnership with them. I had enough money saved, so I'm now part owner of one of the restaurants.

"I made a promise to God that if I ever got a chance at success again, I'd give something back to the street people. Maybe I could be an encouragement to someone, like the pastor was to me. I started handing out burgers every other night. This way, I gave them physical nourishment as well as companionship.

"I've always been open for opportunities to talk with these guys when-ever they want, but I don't push. Success is sometimes slow in terms of people changing their lives, but I'm patient and persistent."

I told Timothy that he was an encouragement to me. There are times when I'm so discouraged and wonder, "Can God do anything here?" Many times just thinking about Timothy has given me the encouragement I needed to continue, knowing that God cares. Timothy is just one example of how God can change a life—of how those on skid row, given another chance, can make it again and become a part of society. For Timothy, success isn't a fancy house or a big car; it's the chance to go out and minister to others.

> *Lord, there are times when we need people like Timothy to come into our lives and bear witness to the fact that You do change lives. Thank You for pastors and others who are working in missions and in places where they receive little recognition or glory. Timothy is a man who loves You and Your perspective. Thank You for his love, persistence, and encouragement to others. Amen.*

Taking It Inward

Never forget these two truths:

- God moves on the hearts of people and draws them to Himself.
- When these people are open to God's moving, they'll be changed.

Timothy had heard the familiar story of the gospel many times, but he remained hard-hearted toward Jesus. God, however, continued to pursue him—and thanks to the gentle encouragement of a discerning pastor who let God do His thing, Timothy's heart softened and he was changed!

In the book of Acts we see God drawing people to Himself and transforming lives by the thousands in just a few days. Acts 8 records one of those transformations—a scene remarkably similar to Timothy's, and one that helps us understand how to **trust God** to change the lives of the people around us.

Read Acts 8:26–40 on the following page. As you read:
- Draw a cloud [☁] over every mention of God; mark any of His representatives—like angels or the Spirit—in the same way.

- Draw an Ichthus [◯✕] over every mention of Philip, a man chosen by the apostles to help with the work of the church. Be sure to mark pronouns like "he."
- Draw a smiley face [☺] over every mention of the Ethiopian. Again, watch for those pronouns!

Acts 8:26–40

26 Now an angel of the Lord said to Philip, "Go south to the road—the desert road—that goes down from Jerusalem to Gaza." 27 So he started out, and on his way he met an Ethiopian eunuch, an important official in charge of all the treasury of Candace, queen of the Ethiopians. This man had gone to Jerusalem to worship, 28 and on his way home was sitting in his chariot reading the book of Isaiah the prophet. 29 The Spirit told Philip, "Go to that chariot and stay near it."

30 Then Philip ran up to the chariot and heard the man reading Isaiah the prophet. "Do you understand what you are reading?" Philip asked.

31 "How can I," he said, "unless someone explains it to me?" So he invited Philip to come up and sit with him. 32 The eunuch was reading this passage of Scripture: "He was led like a sheep to the slaughter, and as a lamb before the shearer is silent, so he did not open his mouth. 33 In his humiliation he was deprived of justice. Who can speak of his descendants? For his life was taken from the earth."

34 The eunuch asked Philip, "Tell me, please, who is the prophet talking about, himself or someone else?" 35 Then Philip began with that very passage of Scripture and told him the good news about Jesus. 36 As they traveled along the road, they came to some water and the eunuch said, "Look, here is water. Why shouldn't I be baptized?"

*³⁸ And he gave orders to stop the chariot. Then both Philip and the eunuch went down into the water and Philip baptized him. ³⁹ When they came up out of the water, the Spirit of the Lord suddenly took Philip away, and the eunuch did not see him again, but went on his way rejoicing. ⁴⁰ Philip, however, appeared at Azotus and traveled about, preaching the gospel in all the towns until he reached Caesarea.

Once you've marked the passage, list what you learn about God, Philip, and the Ethiopian. Make your lists as detailed as possible.

God	Philip	Ethiopian

How would you describe the spiritual condition of the Ethiopian when Philip first met him?

What did Philip do to make this a successful witnessing situation?

What part did God play in this?

---

* Some late manuscripts: **baptized**?" ³⁷ **Philip said, "If you believe with all your heart, you may." The official answered, "I believe that Jesus Christ is the Son of God."**

FRI Day 19

What would clue you in to the fact that God was already working in the life of the Ethiopian before Philip ran up to his chariot?

Seal the Deal

In the space below, write the names of at least three people you know, in whom God may be working.

Look at the options below. Thinking of the people you just listed, check three things you can do to imitate Philip as an effective witness of Jesus Christ. What can you do to be more attentive to the spiritual needs of the people around you?

I could:
- ☐   perk up and listen when friends talk about their struggles;
- ☐   follow up on any questions they ask about God;
- ☐   bring God up in casual conversation whenever it seems natural;
- ☐   let friends approach the subject of faith on their own terms;
- ☐   pray every day for the lost people around me;
- ☐   make myself available for whatever God has in mind.

Do Day

Command them **to do good**, to be rich in good deeds, and to be generous and willing to share.

—1 Timothy 6:18 (emphasis added)

Done **Ministry Activity**

☐ Spend a few minutes today finding phone numbers and contacting ministry organizations in your community. You can find most of these organizations in the yellow pages of your phone book (start by looking under "social service organizations"). Collect the contact information in the chart below, which is organized according to the needs listed in Matthew 25 from Day 16. Ask God to direct you to two or three specific needs. Then make a few phone calls and ask what you can do to help.

Need/ Ministry Outlet	Phone Number	Person I Talked To	What I Can Do to Help
Hungry • Food pantry (many churches have these) • Homeless shelter/soup kitchen			
Stranger (lonely) • Nursing home • A senior adult in your church (call your pastor)			
In need of clothes • Homeless shelter • Single-parent family (call your pastor) • *Red Cross			
Sick • Rehabilitation hospital • Hospital volunteer office			
In prison • Jail chaplain • Juvenile detention center • *Prison Fellowship			

* Ask your pastor for contact information on these organizations or find them on the web.

SAT_{Day} 20

☐ As you witnessed through the lives of Timothy and Philip from Day 19, God is working in the lives of people around you and drawing them to Himself. So, take today to see for yourself how this works. Grab three friends and select two or three inexpensive restaurants where you can eat a light snack or a meal. When the server brings your food, ask for his or her name. Then say, "In a moment we're going to be praying for our food. Is there anything we can pray for you?" Pray for your food and the server's need, eat your meal, and be sure to leave a generous tip! Return the following week and check in on your servers.

Worship

See to it, brothers, that none of you has a sinful, unbelieving heart that turns away from the living God. But **encourage one another daily**, as long as it is called Today, so that none of you may be hardened by sin's deceitfulness.
— Hebrews 3:12–13 (emphasis added)

Take this book to church, and use these pages for taking notes on your worship and learning experiences.

Sunday School
Subject:

Bible passages referred to:

What are at least two things you can begin applying **today** from this lesson?

Worship
Write a prayer (perhaps during the offering time or just before the service begins) that expresses your gratitude for His mercy and grace.

SUN_{Day} 21

Sermon

Subject/Title:

Scripture text:

Key points:

Cool thoughts or observations:

What did God say to you through this sermon?

What is He asking you to change?

Connections

How did God weave together your experiences of the week with your worship and learning today? Take a moment to write down any connections in the space below.

Week 4

Day 22   Family Pictures
Day 23   Everywhere You Look
Day 24   Hot Dogs and Beans
Day 25   The Night of the Gun
Day 26   The College
Day 27   Do Day
Day 28   Worship

Family Pictures

For two years, deserted buildings and covered stoops had been my home. Except for a few brief interludes, I was a Burnside Street regular. I had seen more sadness, hopelessness, and despair in those two years than I had in my entire life, and my relationship with my Lord had grown vastly as a result. I began, however, to feel a tug at my heart that seemed to say I would soon be moving on.

One evening, the frigid night air became more than my light jacket could handle, so I hurried to the nearest halfway house. My heart sank when I saw the locked doors before me and realized I'd arrived too late. Leaning against an adjacent building, shifting the weight on my cold feet from one to the other, I watched as more men arrived, only to find the shelter full. Within thirty minutes, more than a dozen of us had gathered.

One by one we sat down against the building, creating some warmth by sitting close to each other. On a cold night, body heat was a wonderful thing; it was common to see several men packed tightly together to protect themselves from the cold.

Some of the men had bottles of cheap wine or whiskey. They'd drink all they wanted and then pass the bottle to the next guy. It was drinking that helped most of them survive the cold nights. The alcohol didn't make them any warmer, of course; it just killed their sensitivity to the cold. This is why homeless people often freeze to death. They're so drunk they don't realize how cold it really is.

That night most of the faces were familiar to me, though I didn't know all of their names. The bottles passed back and forth among the men as they discussed a fight that had taken place earlier in a nearby bar. I sat quietly, concentrating mostly on keeping warm and surviving the cold night.

MONDay 22

Suddenly, I heard a voice directed at me. The other men perked up as if the voice of God Himself had spoken, and I was intimidated by the sudden attention. Apparently the man speaking to me had quite a reputation on the streets as a cruel tyrant. I'm not sure if the reputation was born out of fear, respect, or both.

The man beside me hit my shoulder. "Hey, Duke is talking to you!"

Seeing by my expression that I had not heard him, Duke repeated, "Around the corner, under the metal pipe sticking out of the building is a sleeping bag. Go get it!"

Running his "errand" would mean losing my place in the huddle, and that irritated me. I shot an angry look at the guy and wanted to tell him to go get it himself. I was as cold as he was. Instead I sighed, responded with a simple "okay," and left my coveted spot in the huddle.

Following Duke's directions, I found a clean, nicely folded sleeping bag under some plastic. My first desire was to find a secluded spot and wrap myself in the warmth of it, but instead I returned to the group of men. Naturally, someone had taken my spot in the huddle. Handing the bag to Duke, I anxiously looked for a place to sit. All eyes were on Duke, wondering, I suppose, if the sleeping bag was going to be shared.

Duke took the bag and told the person next to him, "Move over and make room for the boy." The authority Duke possessed became obvious as the guy did exactly what he was told with no argument. I now had a spot, and it was next to the man with the sleeping bag!

At times the street people display a genuine compassion for each other, as though they're all part of one big family. This was one of those moments. Duke opened up the sleeping bag and stretched it as wide as it would go, making sure everyone's feet were covered. Shuffling closer until everyone was satisfied, we were all settled under "our" sleeping bag.

When I awoke the next morning, my nose felt itchy and numb. I tried to rub it, but my hands were too cold and stiff to cooperate. I began to wonder what bar was open this early to serve some hot, freshly brewed coffee.

I rubbed my hands together for warmth, then reached into my pocket to count my change, trying to figure out how many cups of coffee it would buy. By this time, Duke began to stir, and he asked what I was doing.

"I want to buy my friends a cup of coffee," I replied.

We began to talk, and I told Duke what a great thing he'd done the night before. "We were like a big family, all caring and sharing the benefit of your sleeping bag. Thank you," I said—and I meant it!

As we continued to talk, Duke opened up to me about his family. He told me how he had been a family man who began to drink too much. Before long, he was consistently too drunk to work. Eventually his wife kicked him out of the house.

A man next to us was stirred by our conversation, and he began having thoughts of home. He pulled out some old, ragged pictures of his family. His story was quite similar to Duke's. Alcohol had robbed him of his personal and professional life, so he left for the refuge of skid row, where being drunk would be normal and acceptable.

Soon everyone had something to add to the stories of home. Tears started flowing, and arms hugged and consoled. Observing the mood of the group, Duke said, "Guys, Kurt is going to buy us all coffee at the bar. Let's go where it's warm and talk some more." Not wanting to let go of such warm, sentimental feelings, we passed around the pictures as we walked; our conversation didn't miss a beat.

Pulling out my change as we approached the bar, I realized we were going to be one coffee short. I had enough money for everyone but myself. No one else had money to contribute since they'd spent it on cheap booze the night before.

The bartender passed out the coffee, and I listened as each man related how he'd ended up on skid row. It amazed me how many different things had happened in their lives. But there was one factor common to all of the men, and that was the power that alcohol had over their lives. I was pondering this when someone asked, "Kurt, what about your family?"

I had been so involved in what everyone was saying that the question caught me off guard. Duke added, "Why are you here?" He handed me a cup that had been passed around, each man adding some coffee from his own cup until mine was full.

As I sipped the coffee, I reached into my pocket as if to bring out my family pictures. I had none, but I had my New Testament. I began to tell the men stories of Jesus. I told them about the family of God and how they could become a part of that family by accepting Christ as their personal Savior.

A couple of the men walked away, but most of them listened with great interest and seemed focused on my every word. Several men asked questions and seemed genuinely eager to know more. As I attempted to answer their questions, my eyes were drawn to Duke, who had been quiet and seemed very sad. I asked him if he was all right, and he responded by bursting into tears. He told us how much he missed his family and how he yearned to go back.

The bartender was behind the bar, listening to our entire conversation. But as Duke was talking, he came out and quietly placed a hand on Duke's shoulder to console him.

One of the men spoke up. "Duke, why don't you just call your family and tell them you're sorry and that you want to come home?" The men all nodded their heads, encouraging Duke to make the call. The compassionate bartender offered the use of his office phone. Duke explained sadly that several years had gone by and that the number he had was probably not current. We wouldn't let him make excuses though, and encouraged him to call the number. Duke finally gave a submissive shrug and headed to the back room to give it a try.

He returned after about twenty minutes, and I'll always remember his smile, so full of indescribable happiness. In a voice choked with emotion, he said that his wife told him she had prayed for this day—the day when he would call her asking to come home. This was an answer to her prayers!

The bartender offered to drive Duke home just as soon as we all cleared out of his bar. Duke's street family began to leave, wishing him well, all giving a little advice and a pat on the back. I was no exception. I gave Duke a hug and said my good-byes. I gave him my Bible and we parted ways.

Eventually, God did move me on from Burnside Street, and I never saw Duke again. Many times I've wished that I had gotten his address. But I also pray that someday I'll see Duke and the rest of those men as part of a bigger family— the family of God.

Taking It Inward

Did you notice a common denominator among the members of Kurt's "street family"? They were all gripped by the deception of alcohol. Somewhere along the way, each became convinced that he needed what the bottle offered worse than **true life**!

The scary thing is, we can all be deceived in ways far more subtle than alcohol. Sin can present itself to any one of us as an enticing—even safe!—"experiment." Then, before we know it, we're entrenched. The way **out** is unbelievably harder than the way **in**!

The passage that follows shows clearly how the lure of deception works. After you've read it, journal your responses to the questions that follow.

James 1:14–15

14 but each one is tempted when, by his own evil desire, he is dragged away and enticed.

15 Then, after desire has conceived, it gives birth to sin; and sin, when it is full-grown, gives birth to death.

What tempts each person?

What happens to the one tempted?

According to verse 15, what is the growth process of sin? (Fill in the blanks below.)

_____ ➔ _____ ➔ _____

There are **always** consequences to sin. But there is **always** a way to be restored. Jesus explained how this works to a group of Jewish religious leaders (who incidentally had been accusing Jesus of associating with sinners), using a story to illustrate His explanation. Read the story below, noting three things: 1) the point when deception first entered the scene; 2) the consequences of following the deception; and 3) the moment where you see that there's hope for restoration.

Luke 15:11–24

11 Jesus continued: "There was a man who had two sons. 12 The younger one said to his father, 'Father, give me my share of the estate.' So he divided his property between them. 13 "Not long after that, the younger son got together all he had, set off for a distant country and there squandered his wealth in wild living. 14 After he had spent everything, there was a severe famine in that whole country, and he began to be in need. 15 So he went and hired himself out to a citizen of that country, who sent him to his fields to feed pigs. 16 He longed to fill his stomach with the pods that the pigs were eating, but no one gave him anything.

¹⁷ "When he came to his senses, he said, 'How many of my father's hired men have food to spare, and here I am starving to death! ¹⁸ I will set out and go back to my father and say to him: Father, I have sinned against heaven and against you. ¹⁹ I am no longer worthy to be called your son; make me like one of your hired men.'

²⁰ So he got up and went to his father. "But while he was still a long way off, his father saw him and was filled with compassion for him; he ran to his son, threw his arms around him and kissed him. ²¹ "The son said to him, 'Father, I have sinned against heaven and against you. I am no longer worthy to be called your son.'

²² "But the father said to his servants, 'Quick! Bring the best robe and put it on him. Put a ring on his finger and sandals on his feet. ²³ Bring the fattened calf and kill it. Let's have a feast and celebrate. ²⁴ For this son of mine was dead and is alive again; he was lost and is found.' So they began to celebrate."

There are many parallels between Kurt's story of Duke and Jesus' story of the Prodigal Son. Let's focus on two.

1. At a certain point, both Duke and the Prodigal Son realized the trap they had fallen into—and each had a similar reaction: "I want to go back." Memorize this biblical maxim:

   - Sin takes you farther than you intended to go.
   - You stay longer than you intended to stay.
   - You pay more than you intended to pay.

Has this already happened to you? Are you struggling with a deception that has already taken you farther than you intended to go? If so, in the space below, write these words: I want to go back!

_____

MON_{Day} 22

2. Both Duke and the son had someone at home who was eagerly waiting for their return. And when they finally returned, both were welcomed with unconditional love!

If you've reached a point where you want to restore your relationship with Christ, then return! He's ready to give you a big hug and throw an awesome party!

Seal the Deal

Is there a "Duke" or a "prodigal son" in your life—perhaps a friend who's experiencing the consequences of a deceptive desire? How can you be like Duke's wife—or the father in Jesus' story—and play a part in welcoming this person back? Perhaps you're to play the role Kurt played in sharing the good news of the gospel.

In the space below, jot the name of the friend who's like Duke or the Prodigal Son. Then write something you can do to reach out to this person.

Everywhere You Look

The trip from school to Burnside and back was a long one. When my money ran out, bus rides became scarce, and getting there and back meant walking four hours each way.

I always anticipated great things as I walked to Burnside Street, and I could hardly wait to arrive. Sometimes I'd dig deep into my pockets to see if my meager change had multiplied into bus fare since the last time I looked, but to no avail. I was so impatient, and the walk took so long. Maybe it was my impatience that brought about the lesson of the car accident.

As I walked along one day, still far from skid row, I heard a loud crash. It practically scared me to death, and I ran toward the noise. As I rounded a curve in the road, I saw a car that had crashed into several parked cars before going partway through a fence. Half of the car still stuck out into the road. I was the first to reach the scene, and the driver was already out of the car, stumbling around. Smelling the gasoline pouring from the punctured gas tank, I knew I had to get him away before the whole mess blew up and killed us both. We found a safe place to rest, and I tried to determine how badly the man was hurt.

Sitting beside him, I smelled something very familiar—the smell of stale alcohol. My mind went immediately to skid row and the pungent smell of stale liquor so common to derelicts. Looking closely at the man, I saw the familiar bloodshot eyes. It occurred to me that alcohol was a problem almost everywhere—even in nicer neighborhoods like this one—and that wherever it was, destruction followed.

As the man and I waited for help, it dawned on me that I didn't need to go to skid row to find drunks and drug addicts in need of God's touch. They are in our communities, shopping centers, and workplaces. They live in nice homes and drive nice cars. I stand beside them in line at the grocery store and pass them as I walk on the streets. Burnside had been my arena for ministry, yet I felt the Lord using this accident to show me that there were people everywhere who needed to hear about Him, not just on skid row.

The owners of the damaged cars came out of their homes yelling and shaking their fists. They became even angrier when they looked inside the man's car and saw the empty liquor bottles littering the floorboard. I had to keep them away from the injured man so they wouldn't attack him.

Soon the ambulance and police arrived. The police officer asked for my name and phone number and wrote down all the information I knew about the accident. "Sir," I said, "There sure is a lot of need for love in this world, isn't there?"

He stopped writing his report and replied, "Son, everywhere you look, and every time you turn around, people are crying out for love."

Wow! It was like an angel from God speaking to me. Everywhere I looked, every time I turned around, people were looking for love.

I had another two hours to walk before reaching skid row, and I used the time to contemplate what had taken place. I thought about what the officer had said, and my eyes were suddenly opened to the great need all around me, not only with the derelicts and prostitutes. I noticed frail old ladies in dire need of help carrying their groceries—someone who'd had a flat tire and was struggling to fix it. It was true, I could always find people in need. People who needed love were all around me.

Taking It Inward

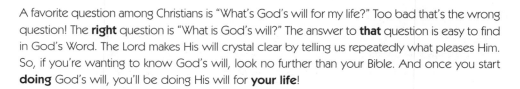

As you read the Bible, you can tell God knew there'd be a shortage of love in this world. Maybe that's why He gave His people so many specific instructions about caring for each other. Kurt and the policeman were experiencing this shortage firsthand. But you've gotta wonder—if more of God's people were obeying His instructions, would we even have such a shortage of love?

A favorite question among Christians is "What's God's will for my life?" Too bad that's the wrong question! The **right** question is "What is God's will?" The answer to **that** question is easy to find in God's Word. The Lord makes His will crystal clear by telling us repeatedly what pleases Him. So, if you're wanting to know God's will, look no further than your Bible. And once you start **doing** God's will, you'll be doing His will for **your life**!

Here are several scriptures that talk about things that please God. As you read them, keep a running list in the margin of things you're told **to do** or **not do**. Notice how many of the things that please God go along with the policeman's observation to Kurt: "Everywhere you look, people are crying out for love."

James 1:27 (NKJV)   **Do/Don't Do**

27 Pure and undefiled religion before God and the Father is this: to visit orphans and widows in their trouble, and to keep oneself unspotted from the world.

Isaiah 1:16–19

16 wash and make yourselves clean. Take your evil deeds out of my sight! Stop doing wrong, 17 learn to do right! Seek justice, encourage the oppressed. Defend the cause of the fatherless, plead the case of the widow. 18 "Come now, let us reason together," says the LORD. "Though your sins are like scarlet, they shall be as white as snow; though they are red as crimson, they shall be like wool. 19 If you are willing and obedient, you will eat the best from the land;"

TUE_{Day} 23

Jeremiah 7:1–7   Do/Don't Do

[1] This is the word that came to Jeremiah from the LORD: [2] "Stand at the gate of the Lord's house and there proclaim this message: "'Hear the word of the LORD, all you people of Judah who come through these gates to worship the LORD. [3] This is what the LORD Almighty, the God of Israel, says: Reform your ways and your actions, and I will let you live in this place. [4] Do not trust in deceptive words and say, "This is the temple of the LORD, the temple of the LORD, the temple of the LORD!"

[5] If you really change your ways and your actions and deal with each other justly, [6] if you do not oppress the alien, the fatherless or the widow and do not shed innocent blood in this place, and if you do not follow other gods to your own harm, [7] then I will let you live in this place, in the land I gave your forefathers for ever and ever.

Micah 6:7–8

[7] Will the LORD be pleased with thousands of rams, with ten thousand rivers of oil? Shall I offer my firstborn for my transgression, the fruit of my body for the sin of my soul? [8] He has showed you, O man, what is good. And what does the LORD require of you? To act justly and to love mercy and to walk humbly with your God.

Now look at your "Do/Don't Do" list. You should have a concise list of practical steps you can take toward pleasing God. In fact, you could think of each as a "baby step" toward doing the will of God.

Think about what you've been up to over the past two months. How do your activities line up with God's "Do/Don't Do" list?

Seal the Deal

Don't close this book without taking a step toward **doing** something you just saw in scripture. Ask the Lord to show you some people in your life (or organizations that minister to people in these circumstances) like those you saw described in the Bible. For example, who are some widows or widowers you know?

Write down the names of these people, then jot down a way you could minister to them over the next week. One more thing: Track down their phone numbers and write them here. This will remind you to get in touch with them soon!

Name   **Ministry Activity**   **Phone Number**

Hot Dogs and Beans

After leaving college, my ministry to the homeless took on a different dimension. That "dimension" is known today as "Church on the Street." Every Thursday night a group of thirty or more folks caravan to the inner-city with bags of clothing, blankets, toiletries, and a food trailer much like the ones carnival vendors use to sell cotton candy and cold drinks.

Our caravan typically winds its way through the narrow city streets until we find a place large enough for everyone to assemble. Sometimes it's an empty parking lot, a city park, or even a sidewalk. Wherever God provides the space, we set up Church on the Street.

It doesn't take long for word to spread among the homeless that someone is serving hot meals, and it's not unusual for us to feed hundreds of men and women in an evening. The food is paid for with donations to the ministry—or we serve donated hot dogs and beans.

On a typical Thursday night, men and women line up for clothing and hot food while our praise team sings familiar hymns like "Amazing Grace." It's not uncommon for the men and women to sing along, some with tears streaming down their faces. Once the food team has satisfied the crowd's physical hunger, the men and women take their seats on plastic chairs and get ready for "church." For many of the homeless, this is the only church they know, and a quiet reverence settles over the whole area. Singing replaces the blaring background noise of the city.

In all the time we've been doing Church on the Street, we've always been blessed with plenty of food to go around—until a night none of us will ever forget. On this particular evening, I was busy setting up sound equipment and preparing for the night's message when Don, a faithful Church on the Street volunteer, approached me with a concerned expression on his face.

"Kurt, we only have five hundred hot dogs tonight," he said.

That may sound like plenty of hot dogs, but lately we'd been attracting hundreds of men and women every Thursday night. We'd always had enough to feed the crowd until everyone was full—and that often meant at least two hot dogs per person. There was no way we could do this with just five hundred hot dogs.

"Why don't we limit each person to one hot dog?" Don suggested.

I understood where he was coming from, but I didn't want anyone to go away hungry.

"Let's go ahead and cook what we have," I told him. "We'll do what we always do and see what happens."

The crowd that night was perhaps the largest we'd attracted all summer. Even if each person took only one hot dog, it was obvious we wouldn't have enough to go around. Ron, the man in charge of our makeshift kitchen, said quietly, "Kurt, we don't have enough. What if we run out and there are hundreds of men left to feed?"

We both knew the situation could quickly escalate into a riot if some people were fed and some were left hungry. Not only was I concerned about feeding everyone, I was also worried about the safety of our volunteers. Though many of our street friends would never have dreamed of being violent, some were capable of stirring up the calmest of crowds. They had no problem at all hurting others in order to get what they wanted.

"What are we going to do?" Ron asked.

"Ron, do the best you can with what you have, and let God do the rest." My words sounded confident, but inside I shared his concern. Ron shook his head and walked away. "We're in trouble," I heard him whisper as he headed back to the kitchen.

A little later Don reported, "We've cooked and served over two hundred guys—two hot dogs and a scoop of beans each. We have about a hundred more hot dogs, and there are still hundreds of people to feed. What do we do?"

"Keep doing what you're doing," I told him before we went back to our posts, still pretending everything was fine.

Later that evening, Don and Ron found me in the crowd. They were nearly breathless with excitement. "We've fed five hundred men, and we still have hot dogs and beans! Where did all this food come from?"

"We may not have had enough food, but God did." My heart overflowed with gratitude toward a loving Father who had apparently multiplied our supply of food so that no one left hungry. It was truly a miracle!

But that's not the end of the story. It seems that God had looked down and noticed one straggler making his way up the sidewalk toward our ministry area. The kitchen team had finished cooking and was busy packing up the trailer as the rest of us prepared for the evening worship service. As the man made his way to the trailer, he looked wistfully at one of our volunteers.

"Do you have any hot dogs left?" he asked.

"I'm so sorry," she told him. "We gave all the food away."

Dejected, the man turned to leave.

"Oh, wait," she said. As the volunteer pulled out the portable stove, she noticed two hot dogs that had apparently fallen beside the stovetop. They were still hot. "Look!" she told the man, "God set these two aside just for you!"

Not only had God multiplied the food for us that summer night; He'd also watched one lonely, hungry man make his way through the city streets in search of something warm to eat. We didn't know it, but He was busy preparing a meal just for that man. God never takes His eyes off His children—not for a second.

As I drove home that night, my heart was bursting with praise for my heavenly Father—a God who loves us so much that He allowed us to glimpse two miracles that night. All He ever asks is that we do our best. He promises to do the rest.

Taking It Inward

We know what you're thinking. There's only one obvious Bible event that parallels the miracle of the hot dogs and beans. And you're right. Jesus' miracle of the five loaves and two fishes (John 6:1–13) is familiar to just about everyone—but few would actually stake their reputation on this miracle as Kurt did!

The engine that powers miracles is faith. Without faith there are no miracles. Let's take a look at two groups of people in scripture—one group that experienced the full benefit of extreme faith, and one group that flat missed out.

To make sure you don't miss the key differences between these two groups, look for the following as you read these passages:

1. Draw a face [☺] over the people—not including Jesus—mentioned.

2. Draw a light bulb [💡] over the word "faith." Draw a "do not" symbol [🚫] over the word "unbelief."

Matthew 13:53–58 (NKJV)

[53] Now it came to pass, when Jesus had finished these parables, that He departed from there. [54] And when He had come to His own country, He taught them in their synagogue, so that they were astonished and said, "Where did this Man get this wisdom and these mighty works? [55] "Is this not the carpenter's son? Is not His mother called Mary? And His brothers James, Joses, Simon, and Judas? [56] "And His sisters, are they not all with us? Where then did this Man get all these things?" [57] So they were offended at Him. But Jesus said to them, "A prophet is not without honor except in his own country and in his own house." [58] Now He did not do many mighty works there because of their unbelief.

Hebrews 11:6–10 (NKJV)

[6] But without faith it is impossible to please Him, for he who comes to God must believe that He is, and that He is a rewarder of those who diligently seek Him. [7] By faith Noah, being divinely warned of things not yet seen, moved with godly fear, prepared an ark for the saving of his household, by which he condemned the world and became heir of the righteousness which is according to faith. [8] By faith Abraham obeyed when he was called to go out to the place which he would receive as an inheritance. And he went out, not knowing where he was going. [9] By faith he dwelt in the land of promise as in a foreign country, dwelling in tents with Isaac and Jacob, the heirs with him of the same promise; [10] for he waited for the city which has foundations, whose builder and maker is God.

Now let's compare and contrast the people in these two passages. Circle the phrases below that you think describe the faith of the people in the Matthew passage.

solid   non-existent
weak   existent but not in working order
distracted   a good example to imitate
focused   not a good example to imitate

Circle the phrases that you think describe the faith of the people in the Hebrews passage.

solid	non-existent
weak	existent but not in working order
distracted	a good example to imitate
focused	not a good example to imitate

What did the people around Jesus in the Matthew passage miss out on because of their unbelief?

What did the people in the Hebrews passage get to experience because of their faith?

What were the people with Jesus (in Matthew) paying attention to?

Look at the faces you drew in the Hebrews passage. What were these people focused on?

Think for a second how Kurt's story might have ended had he not decided to trust God. People would have been sent away…the hot dogs would have been rationed…no one would have eaten until he was full…and no miracle ("mighty works") would have occurred because of their unbelief. It would have been a frustrating, discouraging night. Instead, God was glorified—and we have the benefit of an incredible story.

Seal the Deal

What's going on in your life that can only be explained by the mighty works of God? Are you ready to stake your reputation on a step of faith? Or would you rather have Matthew 13:58 describe your life? Check this out:

> Now Jesus did not do many mighty works in the life of _____ (insert your name) because of his/her unbelief.

God may be putting some things in your life that can be great opportunities to exercise "hot dogs and beans" faith. Take a minute to brainstorm about these. We'll get you started with a few suggestions—but be sure to ask the Holy Spirit for His.

☐   Changing your heart toward someone who has hurt you.

☐   Mobilizing your youth group to help or start a ministry in your community (such as helping at a nursing home or homeless shelter, or starting an after-school program for kids).

☐   Launching a Christian club on your school campus.

☐   Raising funds for an important cause or ministry.

The Night of the Gun

The ministry team arrived at the parking lot around 6 P.M., just as they had done many times before. It was a beautiful sunny evening—quite ordinary in every sense. As usual, hundreds of men and women were already waiting inside the gated area. Some of the team were in the process of parking their cars outside the lot. Others were taking stoves out of the trailer, placing water barrels out for drinks, and setting up the sound system for our Church on the Street service.

One of the first items on our agenda is to distribute cookies and cakes while things are being set up; it creates a welcoming atmosphere for our guests. So one of the team workers, a woman, eagerly began to give out cookies at the gate.

But this night the crowd seemed agitated—and before long they mobbed the woman, as if fearing that the cookies would run out before they could get some.

"They're acting like this is their last meal," I thought in amazement. Seeing that the woman was in trouble, I headed for the middle of the mob and grabbed the cookies to draw their attention away from her. In my haste to reach her, I accidentally pushed aside several men. One of the men erupted in anger and began yelling profanities and making obscene gestures at me. I responded with a hug, trying to soften his anger by telling him I loved him.

Just then, the man took a pistol out of his jacket. Shoving it into my chest so hard that it left a bruise, he threatened, "I am so mad at you and the world, Pastor Kurt. You will no longer be able to tell anyone how to find happiness in Jesus—no one!"

For a second I was stunned. Then, almost instantly, God moved on me to speak to the man. "You cannot shoot me unless God allows it," I said. "You see, you are not in control here. God is. And furthermore, if God does allow you to shoot me, you will have nowhere to run. God will know every hiding place and every corner you run to."

Though I faced the man with uncharacteristic courage, in truth I was more mad than scared. Still holding the gun to my chest, he glared at me hatefully. I could almost hear the wheels of his mind turning—processing the fact that he'd backed himself into a corner. In fear and desperation, he pulled the trigger.

The gun did not go off.

The man looked stunned—then puzzled. He cursed again and dropped the gun. As he sauntered away I heard him yell, "Your God can have the gun!"

It seemed as if time had stopped. But as I looked around me, I became aware that the world hadn't stopped turning. In fact, the majority of people were unaware of what had just happened. The crowd was lining up for the evening meal. The staff was still busy setting up the portable kitchen. The ministry team was anticipating the great things the Lord would do that evening.

I encouraged the few who had witnessed the event to keep working as if nothing had happened. But before getting back to my tasks, I picked up the gun, stuck it in my shirt, and went into a portable toilet to examine it.

What I found there astounded me. Every chamber of the gun contained a bullet. There was no reason for it not to have fired—except that it wasn't in God's plan.

Instead of a gunshot, the words of Isaiah 54:17 seemed to resound through the evening air: *"No weapon formed against you shall prosper..."*

Taking It Inward

Although it doesn't seem like it at times, God **really** is in control. His Word says so. Over and over in scripture, God reminds us that He's with us—just as He was with Kurt when the trigger of the gun was pulled.

God knew His people would face a constant battle in this fallen world. Perhaps that's why the Bible has so much to say about God's help and protection in times of trouble. Take a look at several passages that assure us of God's protection and help, printed below. Carefully meditate on these verses and allow yourself to be touched by God's presence—in fact, take this book, your Bible, and a pen to a quiet place where you can be alone with the Lord. As you meditate on these verses, journal in the margin your thoughts about these two things:

- any guarantees of protection from God;
- the attitudes or behavior of the people following God.

Isaiah 54:17a (NKJV)

17 No weapon formed against you shall prosper...

Psalm 91:1–6 (NKJV)

1 He who dwells in the secret place of the Most High Shall abide under the shadow of the Almighty. 2 I will say of the LORD, "He is my refuge and my fortress; My God, in Him I will trust." 3 Surely He shall deliver you from the snare of the fowler And from the perilous pestilence. 4 He shall cover you with His feathers, And under His wings you shall take refuge; His truth shall be your shield and buckler. 5 You shall not be afraid of the terror by night, Nor of the arrow that flies by day, 6 Nor of the pestilence that walks in darkness, Nor of the destruction that lays waste at noonday.

Psalm 112:1–10 (NKJV)

¹ Praise the LORD! Blessed is the man who fears the LORD, Who delights greatly in His commandments. ² His descendants will be mighty on earth; The generation of the upright will be blessed. ³ Wealth and riches will be in his house, And his righteousness endures forever. ⁴ Unto the upright there arises light in the darkness; He is gracious, and full of compassion, and righteous. ⁵ A good man deals graciously and lends; He will guide his affairs with discretion. ⁶ Surely he will never be shaken; The righteous will be in everlasting remembrance. ⁷ He will not be afraid of evil tidings; His heart is steadfast, trusting in the LORD. ⁸ His heart is established; He will not be afraid, Until he sees his desire upon his enemies. ⁹ He has dispersed abroad, He has given to the poor; His righteousness endures forever; His horn will be exalted with honor. ¹⁰ The wicked will see it and be grieved; He will gnash his teeth and melt away; The desire of the wicked shall perish.

1 Peter 3:8–14

⁸ Finally, all of you be of one mind, having compassion for one another; love as brothers, be tenderhearted, be courteous; ⁹ not returning evil for evil or reviling for reviling, but on the contrary blessing, knowing that you were called to this, that you may inherit a blessing. ¹⁰ For "He who would love life And see good days, Let him refrain his tongue from evil, And his lips from speaking deceit. ¹¹ Let him turn away from evil and do good; Let him seek peace and pursue it. ¹² For the eyes of the LORD are on the righteous, And His ears are open to their prayers; But the face of the LORD is against those who do evil." ¹³ And who is he who will harm you if you become followers of what is good? ¹⁴ But even if you should suffer for righteousness' sake, you are blessed. "And do not be afraid of their threats, nor be troubled."

Hebrews 13:5–6 (NKJV)

⁵ Let your conduct be without covetousness; be content with such things as you have. For He Himself has said, "I will never leave you nor forsake you." ⁶ So we may boldly say: "The LORD is my helper; I will not fear. What can man do to me?"

Look back at the attitudes and behavior of the people in these passages. What traits do you see that you can imitate? What commands do you see that you can obey?

Seal the Deal

The statements below reflect two types of people: those who live in fear and don't trust God's protection, and those who trust God's protection and live with confidence. As you read these statements, underline the ones that describe you. Circle the ones you want to aspire to.

I fear bad news.

God is my helper; I know that no one can harm me.

I worry a lot about what other people think of me.

I'm not content with what I have (clothes, looks, etc.).

I know that the eyes of God are on me and that He's listening for my prayers.

I'm blessed even if I do suffer for being righteous.

My heart is steadfast because I trust in God.

I struggle with being bold in my faith at school.

I worry more than I pray.

THU_{Day} 25

Write on a note card all the statements you circled. Tape this on your bathroom mirror or on a school notebook—or hang it from your rearview mirror. Wherever you put it, be reminded of these precepts every day. You may want to reread the Scriptures above and add to your list. But be sure to do more than **aspire** to these precepts…**own** them!

The College

I'm deeply grateful for the years I spent on skid row while a student at Warner Pacific College, though at times the two environments created conflict in my life. When I first went to college, I didn't intend to have a ministry with street people, but I began to feel a strong calling to it. My desire to attend Warner Pacific was just as strong. Without great student friendships, a group of supportive professors, and clear direction from God, my ministry on skid row would not have been possible.

Because I had struggled to get through high school, I knew I would need a lot of personal attention to succeed in college, and Warner Pacific was known as a close-knit school with a low teacher-student ratio. The professors took a personal interest in their students' lives. In addition, it was a highly regarded Christian college with excellent academic credentials.

In the beginning, I was much like any ordinary college freshman. But as I sensed the strong urge to minister to street people, the demands of college life and the ministry came into conflict. Dorm rules required that I be in by midnight, yet often I wouldn't return to the dorm for a week at a time while I lived on the street. I didn't get my assignments completed on time, and priorities were difficult for me to establish.

After being on the streets for a number of months, I was arrested and put in jail. I wasn't guilty of any wrongdoing; I was simply in the wrong place at the wrong time—a common occurrence on skid row. The officer who processed my paperwork became my sole supporter within the police department. He was usually the one who greeted me after subsequent arrests during my ministry. Not wanting me to get hurt, he did all he could to keep me off the streets. Finally, out of concern for my welfare, he phoned the dean of students—a call that could have ended my ministry on skid row or caused me to be kicked out of school.

One evening when I returned to campus, a note was waiting from the dean. I knew the news would not be good. After cleaning myself up, I went to meet my doom. I prayed each step of the way, wondering how the dean would react to my latest arrest. I also wondered how I would be able to continue my education *and* my ministry, to which I strongly believed God had called me. The dean's message was short and to the point. He placed me on probation, warning that if I violated the dorm rules again or were arrested for anything, it would mean my immediate dismissal from school.

My roommates and two support families were the only ones aware of my ministry on skid row. After telling them about my dilemma, I asked them to pray that God would give me a clear direction of what to do. Within the week, I received another message to meet with the dean. As I went to see him, I prayed along the way.

When I arrived at his office, the dean said without any explanation, "You can go to Burnside on your own, as long as you don't tell anybody." He also told me that if my schoolwork suffered, he would be forced to suspend me. I left his office smiling from ear to ear, once again in total awe of the workings of God. Now I could continue to be obedient to both of God's calls, college and street ministry.

I am deeply grateful for professors like Dr. Orr and others who allowed me to do many "independent studies" and tutored me while I was in school. I spent many nights in their homes while they helped prepare me for the next days' tests.

I'm also thankful for students like Rick, Fred, Debbie, and many others who were my support group. They stayed up countless nights to pray on my behalf. They listened, hugged, laughed, and cried with me. They helped type my papers, helped me understand difficult class subjects, and most of all, believed in what God could do through me.

Warner Pacific College, my professors, and my friends believed in me. I thank God for the school and for the emotional and spiritual growth I experienced while there. To God be the glory!

Taking It Inward

God never intended for His workers to work alone. Kurt could not have accomplished what he did on the streets of Portland without the help and encouragement of many people. If you've considered diving into any kind of ministry—whether you're launching an organization or taking a plate of cookies to a widow—ask for help!

Just after Jesus was here on earth, God used Paul to plant several new churches, as well as to write encouraging letters to these churches to help keep them on track. Today, these letters make up much of the New Testament. Paul was a busy man who accomplished a lot for God. But he didn't do it alone! In fact, he had loads of help.

At the close of Paul's letters, he'd often take a paragraph or two just to thank folks or ask his readers to pass along warm regards. The longest of these "thank you notes" is the last chapter of Romans. Most of this chapter is printed below. As you read it, circle every name you see, and underline anything Paul said about that person.

Romans 16:1–15

1 I commend to you our sister Phoebe, a servant of the church in Cenchrea. 2 I ask you to receive her in the Lord in a way worthy of the saints and to give her any help she may need from you, for she has been a great help to many people, including me.

3 Greet Priscilla and Aquila, my fellow workers in Christ Jesus. 4 They risked their lives for me. Not only I but all the churches of the Gentiles are grateful to them. 5 Greet also the church that meets at their house. Greet my dear friend Epenetus, who was the first convert to Christ in the province of Asia.

⁶ Greet Mary, who worked very hard for you. ⁷ Greet Andronicus and Junias, my relatives who have been in prison with me. They are outstanding among the apostles, and they were in Christ before I was. ⁸ Greet Ampliatus, whom I love in the Lord. ⁹ Greet Urbanus, our fellow worker in Christ, and my dear friend Stachys. ¹⁰ Greet Apelles, tested and approved in Christ. Greet those who belong to the household of Aristobulus. ¹¹ Greet Herodion, my relative. Greet those in the household of Narcissus who are in the Lord.

¹² Greet Tryphena and Tryphosa, those women who work hard in the Lord. Greet my dear friend Persis, another woman who has worked very hard in the Lord. ¹³ Greet Rufus, chosen in the Lord, and his mother, who has been a mother to me, too. ¹⁴ Greet Asyncritus, Phlegon, Hermes, Patrobas, Hermas and the brothers with them. ¹⁵ Greet Philologus, Julia, Nereus and his sister, and Olympas and all the saints with them.

Paul specifically mentioned six people who did work for God, either with him or in general. Find these people and write their names below. Also record Paul's descriptions of them.

Name   **Description**

What does this teach you about what God expects of His workers?

We really do need each other! Read the following passages from your Bible. As you read, jot down everything you learn about helping one other in ministry. By the way, don't forget to apply it to yourself!

1 Thessalonians 3:1–3   **Hebrews 3:12–13**   **Hebrews 10:24–25**

Seal the Deal

You may not be called to Zimbabwe or to the streets of Portland, but you can easily come alongside those who are. The call to help is as important as the call to go. The "goers" can't be effective without the "helpers."

How can you help? Who's doing ministry around you that needs help? Here are some ideas to get your wheels turning, but don't let them limit your thinking. Think big! Think small! Think world-wide! Think city-wide!

Place/Person	Possible Tasks
• A church youth pastor or volunteer worker	• Making phone calls; sending notes; running errands; picking up supplies; laying out a newsletter; assisting in ministry activities
• Your senior pastor	• Running errands; helping with hospital visits
• A local ministry (i.e., a homeless shelter or food pantry)	• Stuffing envelopes; helping with clean-up; running errands; grocery shopping
• A national ministry headquartered near you	• Answering phones; offering office help

Do Day

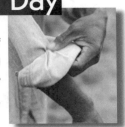

Suppose a brother or sister is without clothes and daily food. If one of you says to him, "Go, I wish you well; keep warm and well fed," but does nothing about his physical needs, what good is it? In the same way, faith by itself, **if it is not accompanied by action,** is dead.

—James 2:15–17 (emphasis added)

Done   **Ministry Activity**

☐   Do exactly what James 1:27 (from Day 23) says to do—visit an orphan or widow in trouble. You may personally know a child who has lost a parent (or parents) or someone who has lost a spouse. If not, call your pastor for some suggestions. Then think one of two ways:

1. Do something for them (like washing their car or mowing their grass), or;

2. Ask them to help you do something for someone else (like baking some cookies or fixing a meal).

CAUTION: Don't make this a one-time deal! Allow for the possibility that this may grow into a long-lasting friendship.

☐   Take a step—giant or baby—toward mobilizing an ongoing ministry. Call your youth leader or an adult friend and share your ideas. We've listed some thought-starters below. As you decide on the step you're going to take, keep one thing in mind: Stake your reputation on God's help, just as Kurt did with the hot dogs and beans (Day 24). Let your ministry show the mighty works of God!

- Organize volunteers to help on a regular basis with any of the following: serving at a local children's hospital, Ronald McDonald House, or summer food program.

- Launch an after-school program for children in your church's neighborhood.

- Supply volunteers to consistently help a ministry in your community (for example, a nursing home, a homeless shelter, a food pantry, or a soup kitchen).

- Start a Bible study or Christian club on your school campus. Or, simply help existing clubs work together.

☐ Do you remember from Day 26 (The College) how many people helped Kurt with his work? Do you recall how many helped the apostle Paul? Write down the name of someone in ministry whom you'd like to help. Call that person right now. (Go ahead, put down the book and do it!) Schedule a time when you can help that person with **anything**…washing the car, grocery shopping, helping with projects, running errands, or babysitting (for free!).

Worship

Let the word of Christ dwell in you richly as you **teach and admonish one another** with all wisdom, and as you **sing psalms, hymns and spiritual songs with gratitude in your hearts to God**.
—Colossians 3:16 (emphasis added)

Take this book to church, and use these pages for taking notes on your worship and learning experiences today.

Sunday School
Subject:

Bible passages referred to:

What are at least two things you can begin applying **today** from this lesson?

Worship
Write a prayer (perhaps during the offering time or just before the service begins) that expresses your gratitude for His mercy and grace.

SUN_{Day} 28

Sermon

Subject/Title:

Scripture text:

Key points:

Cool thoughts or observations:

What did God say to you through this sermon?

What is He asking you to change?

Connections

How did God weave together your experiences of the week with your worship and learning today? Take a moment to write down any connections in the space below.

Bonus Days

Day 29   A Day Away with God
Day 30   Say Yes to Mercy

A Day Away with God

Through Kurt's stories you've seen Jesus' immeasurable mercy in action. As you've studied the scriptures, you've seen that Kurt was simply taking God at His Word. What about you? What's God saying to you? Is He calling you to a life of immeasurable mercy? Are you taking God at His Word?

Use today, Day 29, to put a giant exclamation point on your experience with this book. Schedule an entire day to be with God. Take a personal day off work; use a school holiday or a summer vacation day. Go to a quiet place like the woods, a park, a beach, a library, or your church sanctuary. Arrive early and stay late. Find a place where you can linger with God for a long time without distractions.

Here are some things to take along with you and do when you get there.

To Take:

• Your Bible (God speaks through His Word.)

• A pen and a journal (When He speaks, you'd better write it down.)

• This book (When you review your notes and thoughts, you may be surprised to see how much God has been speaking to you as you've read the stories and studied His Word.)

To Do:

These activities are simply suggestions. The main idea is to submit yourself to God's activities.

1. When you get to the place where you're spending the day, spend some time quieting and cleansing your heart. Meditate on these passages:

Psalm 66:17–20; 2 Chronicles 7:13–15; Jeremiah 29:13; and 1 John 1:8–9.

2. Review each day of this book. Revisit Kurt's stories, read any notes you made, and review the "Seal the Deal" exercise from each study.

- Each of Kurt's stories presents a unique set of circumstances. Which circumstances touch your heart the most?

- In what areas of life are you experiencing conviction from God?

- What is He challenging you to do?

3. Keep listening to God. Pick a day from the book and memorize the scriptures you studied that day.

4. Renew your experience with Jesus' life. Many of the passages you've studied in this book are from the gospel of John. Fill in the gaps by carefully reading the entire gospel of John as if you've never read it before (it won't take as long as you think). But do more than simply read the book; pay attention to detail. After you read each chapter, summarize what you saw by jotting in a notebook things like location, time, people, their actions, any commands or promises, and so on. This will help you listen intently for God's voice.

5. As you wind down your time alone with God, picture the life of mercy you want to live. Be courageous and bold in determining what needs to change so that you can live out the mercy you picture.

Say Yes to Mercy

Okay. On Day 29 we told you to put an exclamation point on your experience with this book. But that's not really the punctuation we'd like to leave you with! An exclamation point is too final. A colon (:) would be more like it. The reason? A colon indicates that something follows. And that's what God wants to happen as a result of what you've read.

To make sure something follows, we invite you to get in touch with us (us being Kurt and Barry). Listed below are the web sites of Church on the Street (where Kurt ministers) and InWord (where Barry ministers). You can post a bulletin board note or send an e-mail from either site.

Tell us what God has shown you and how He has changed you in your experience with **Mercy Beyond Measure**. Type in a paragraph or two of your commitments, challenges, and convictions. Then click "submit" (on the web page and in your heart). Let this be your first step in living a life of reckless grace and mercy beyond measure.

www.churchonthestreet.com
www.inword.org

Topical Index

Belief in Jesus
Day 24

Comfort
Day 1
Day 12
Day 17

Compassion
Day 17
Day 23

Contentment
Day 25

Death
Day 3

Deception
Day 15
Day 22

Decision Making
Day 1

Encouragement
Day 4
Day 9

Encouraging Others
Day 9
Day 26

Evil
Day 5
Day 11

Faith
Day 24
Day 25

Friendship
Day 4
Day 9
Day 26

Giving
Day 4
Day 8

God's Call
Day 1
Introduction

God's Control
Day 5
Day 12

God's Love
Day 12

God's Protection
Day 11
Day 25

God's Will
Day 23

Grace
Day 2
Day 10
Day 15
Day 22

Guidance
Day 1

Guilt
Day 10

Helping Others
Day 19
Day 26

Loving Others
Day 3
Day 9
Day 16
Day 17
Day 23

Loving the Unlovable
Day 16
Introduction

Materialism
Day 8

Mercy
Day 4
Day 17
Day 23

Obedience
Day 16
Day 18
Day 19

Prayer
Day 16
Day 18
Day 24

Rejecting God
Day 2

Salvation
Day 2
Day 10
Day 15

Sharing Your Faith
Day 2
Day 18
Day 19

Sin
Day 22

Temptation
Day 11
Day 15
Day 22

Tough Times
Day 3
Day 5
Day 11

Transformation
Day 10

Unconditional Love
Day 3
Day 8

Why Bad Things Happen
Day 5
Day 12

Worry
Day 8

Scripture Index

Scripture Reference, Page Number

Genesis 12,   11
Genesis 16:1–14,   11–12
Genesis 37:3–5,   41
Genesis 37:23–24,   41
Genesis 37:36,   42
Genesis 39:2–4,   42
Genesis 39:7–18,   42
Genesis 39:19–21,   42
Genesis 41:15–16,   42
Genesis 41:17–38,   42
Genesis 41:39–41,   43
Genesis 42:1–7,   43
Genesis 42:8,   43
Genesis 45:1–3,   43
Genesis 50:18–20,   43
Genesis 50:20,   44

Psalm 91:1–6,   173
Psalm 112:1–10,   174

Proverbs 14:31,   121

Ecclesiastes 4:9–10,   34

Isaiah 1:16–19,   159
Isaiah 54:17a,   173

Jeremiah 7:1–7,   160

Micah 6:7–8,   160

Malachi 3:10,   57

Matthew 3:16–4:1,   73
Matthew 5:43–48,   116
Matthew 9:35–38,   122
Matthew 13:53–58,   167
Matthew 14:13–14,   122

Matthew 25:31–46,   115–16
Matthew 25:32–36,   117

Mark 6:34,   123

Luke 7:12–15,   123
Luke 10:29–37,   122
Luke 12:22–40,   55–56
Luke 12:28,   57
Luke 15:11–24,   154–55

John 2:22,   107
John 3:1–16,   18–19
John 3:10–16,   21
John 3:10–18,   105–06
John 4:39,   107
John 7:43–53,   19
John 8:3–11,   67–68
John 8:23–24,   106
John 9:35–38,   107
John 11:25–27,   107
John 13:34–35,   29
John 15:10–14,   29
John 16:32–33,   74
John 16:33,   88
John 19:38–42,   19–20

Acts 8:26–40,   139–41
Acts 12:1–11,   86–87

Romans 3:21–26,   68
Romans 5:1–9,   68
Romans 12:1–2,   69
Romans 12:10–13,   34
Romans 16:1–15,   179–80

1 Corinthians 3:1–11,   132
1 Corinthians 3:8–11,   134

2 Corinthians 1:3–4,   87
2 Corinthians 1:3–5,   13
2 Corinthians 3:17–18,   69

Ephesians 1:17–21,   21
Ephesians 3:13–21,   44
Ephesians 5:19–20,   91
Ephesians 6:10–12,   75
Ephesians 6:13–20,   76

Colossians 1:9–14,   21
Colossians 3:16,   185

1 Thessalonians 3:1–3,   181
1 Thessalonians 5:11–14,   61

1 Timothy 6:18,   143

Titus 3:3–7,   68

Hebrews 3:12–13,   145, 181
Hebrews 3:12–19,   61
Hebrews 10:23–25,   62
Hebrews 10:24,   89
Hebrews 10:24–25,   47, 181
Hebrews 11:6–10,   167
Hebrews 13:1–3,   34
Hebrews 13:5–6,   175

James 1:1–4,   44
James 1:14–15,   154
James 1:22,   45
James 1:27,   159
James 2:15–17,   183

1 Peter 3:8–14,   174

1 John 4:7–15,   30

About the Authors

Kurt Salierno is dedicated to serving wherever Jesus would serve—giving of his time, comfort, and resources to provide for the needs of homeless men, alcoholics, and prostitutes. Having ministered in the inner-city for many years (this includes sleeping in garbage bins and under bridges), Kurt recently founded and directs Church on the Street in Atlanta. An ordained minister and former youth pastor, Kurt now serves as a "pastor to the street"—providing shelter, food, and the gospel message to hundreds each week. He and his wife, Lori, live in Atlanta, Georgia.

Barry Shafer has run the gamut in youth ministry—from volunteer director to full-time church youth pastor. In his years of connecting with teen spirituality, Barry has developed a passion for helping teens and young adults experience God in invigorating ways through His Word. Barry launched and directs InWord Resources, a ministry dedicated to producing in-depth Bible studies that engage student small-groups in meaningful experiences with scripture.

As a writer, teacher, and conference leader, Barry advances biblical literacy by helping youth workers overcome barriers that inhibit effective Bible study in youth ministry. He and his wife, Dana, live in Middletown, Ohio.

Inner-City Ministry

Church on the Street is a ministry committed to feeding the hungry, clothing the naked, and giving hope to the hopeless in the inner-city of Atlanta. **You can schedule a mission trip** with Church on the Street and minister to the hundreds of poor and homeless with whom Kurt and his staff work every day. You'll build relationships with the poor and help meet their needs while learning ministry skills you'll have for the rest of your life.

Your mission trip can include:
- Bible day camps
- soup kitchen
- clothing distribution
- city clean-up
- paint and repair homeless shelters
- goody bag distribution
- ministry teams

www.churchonthestreet.com
770/966-1216

Kurt Salierno
Church on the Street
P.O. Box 1868
Kennesaw, GA 30156
e-mail: ksalierno@churchonthestreet.com

Small-Group Bible Studies

InWord Resources is a ministry dedicated to equipping teens, youth workers, and young adults with God's Word. InWord's small-group Bible studies incorporate teen-tested inductive study tools and the type of wholehearted seeking that guarantees results! Each study contains an invigorating leader prep, as well as reproducible student sheets for group members. InWord's studies are ideal for discipleship groups, campus Bible studies, and weekend retreats. Visit InWord's web site or call for a free catalog.

www.inword.org
888/422-3060

Barry Shafer
InWord Resources
P.O. Box 531
Middletown, OH 45042
e-mail: info@inword.org